Holy Writ as Oral Lit

Holy Writ as Oral Lit

The Bible as Folklore

Alan Dundes

ROWMAN & LITTLEFIELD PUBLISHERS, INC.
Lanham • Boulder • New York • Oxford

ROWMAN & LITTLEFIELD PUBLISHERS, INC.

Published in the United States of America
by Rowman & Littlefield Publishers, Inc.
4720 Boston Way, Lanham, Maryland 20706

12 Hid's Copse Road
Cumnor Hill, Oxford OX2 9JJ, England

British Library Cataloguing in Publication Information Available

Library of Congress Cataloging-in-Publication Data

Dundes, Alan.
    Holy writ as oral lit : the Bible as folklore / Alan Dundes.
        p.   cm.
    Includes bibliographical references and index.
    ISBN 0-8476-9197-7 (alk. paper). — ISBN 0-8476-9198-5 (pbk. :
alk. paper)
    1. Folklore in the Bible.   2. Bible—Criticism, Form.   I. Title.
BS625.D86   1999
220.6'6—dc21   98-42449
                                                            CIP

Printed in the United States of America

♾ ™ The paper used in this publication meets the minimum requirements of
American National Standard for Information Sciences—Permanence of Paper
for Printed Library Materials, ANSI Z39.48-1984.

Contents

Acknowledgments

This book combines a lifelong love of the Bible with a career in the study of folklore. The numerous citations all come from my family Bible, which happens to be the King James Version, first set forth in 1611. I am well aware of the existence of many different translations of the Bible besides the Authorized Version of 1611, such as the Revised Standard Version of 1952 and the Jerusalem Bible of 1966. I do not believe that the validity of my argument depends upon using any one particular translation of the Bible. The argument stands or falls on its own merit; minor differences in the wording of any passage in either the Old or the New Testament should not affect the basic thrust of my discussion.

I would like to express my heartfelt thanks to my dear wife, Carolyn, who has encouraged me in this as in all my scholarly endeavors, and especially for repeatedly asking, Isn't all this already pretty much known by readers of the Bible? Is there anything new or original in what you are saying? It is my sincere hope that readers of this book will answer those questions, respectively, "No" and "Yes!"

Alan Dundes

Holy Writ as Oral Lit:
The Bible as Folklore

All Scripture is given by inspiration of God. (2 Tim. 3:16)

In 1918, James George Frazer published his three-volume work entitled *Folklore in the Old Testament.* In this milestone of comparative folklore scholarship, Frazer sought to demonstrate that there were parallels to various narratives and customs in the Old Testament. Nearly one entire volume of the three was devoted, for example, to citing versions of the flood myth from all over the world. Frazer said nothing, though, about possible folklore parallels to the contents of the New Testament. It was one thing to suggest that the Jewish component of the Bible had innumerable parallels among savage and peasant peoples; it was quite another to hint at the possible nonuniqueness of the Christian component. There is additional anecdotal evidence supporting the idea that the Old Testament contained folklore content. According to one source (Schneeweis 1983:149), Leopold Schmidt, a leading Austrian folklorist of the twentieth century, would often begin his lectures on folklore with the following: "If someone asks me what he should read as an introduction to folklore, then I say to him, 'Read Homer and the Old Testament!' " In any event, Romanian rabbi and folklorist Moses Gaster reviewed Frazer's volumes favorably in the English journal *Folklore* in 1919. His review included the following praise: "It is refreshing to find now a master in the science of Folklore trying his hand and bringing Folklore to the Bible and not making the Bible Folklore" (Gaster 1919:72). I hope to show that Gaster was mistaken, because I intend to demonstrate that the Bible is indeed folklore. And,

1

I might add, it is not a question of "making" the Bible folklore; it *is* folklore. Once the nature or definition of bona fide folklore is made clear, it will become obvious that the Bible clearly manifests the basic distinctive criteria of folklore: namely, multiple existence and variation.

What Is Folklore?

Since there is often confusion about exactly what folklore is or is not, let me clarify the definition. Folklore is, first of all, not a synonym for error or fallacy, as in the common phrase "That's just folklore." This is not what folklore means to the professional folklorist. (In the same way, "myth" is not a synonym for error or fallacy but is rather a sacred narrative explaining how the world and humankind came to be in their present form. Myth is one genre out of several hundred genres of folklore.) Folklore is distinguishable from so-called high or elite culture and from popular culture on a number of grounds. Almost all high and popular culture exist in fixed, unchanging form either because a novel or short story is locked into print or a television program or motion picture is locked into videotape or film. Every time one reads a Faulkner novel, it is the same, and it will be the same centuries from now; the same holds for television reruns or movies. Audiences may change, but the text, so to speak, cannot really change to any extent. (I am not talking about the colorization of black and white films.) In contrast, folklore is always in flux, always changing. Because of the factors of multiple existence and variation, no two versions of an item of folklore will be identical.

Sometimes the variation will be slight; in other instances, it may be considerable. By slight, I mean it can come down to a single word or a single sentence. For example, take the proverb "A friend in need is a friend indeed." When enunciated orally, it is not always possible to distinguish that version from "A friend in need is a friend in deed." The short pause, or "plus juncture" as it is termed in linguistics, between "in" and "deed" may be difficult to discern. Yet there may be subtle differences in meaning. The first version simply asserts that someone who helps a person when that person needs help is truly (indeed) a friend. The second version seems to argue that a true friend is one who acts, that is, performs an actual deed, rather than just offering mere words to someone in distress.

In folkloristics, we distinguish between free-phrase genres (such as legends and jokes in which the plot is traditional but the wording may vary) and fixed-phrase genres (such as folk similes or tongue twisters in which both the content and the wording are traditional). Fixed-phrase genres also manifest multiple existence and variation. Molasses whose sticky viscosity makes it pour very slowly has inspired the folk simile "as slow as molasses." Variants include "as slow as molasses in January," "as slow as molasses in January flowing uphill," and "as slow as molasses in January flowing uphill in a blizzard." Tongue twisters show similar variation. "The sea ceaseth and sufficeth us" can also appear as "The seething sea ceaseth and so sufficeth us" or even "The seething sea ceaseth and thus the seething sea sufficeth us." Another common tongue twister playing upon the alternation of the /s/ and /sh/ sounds is "I slit a sheet." Other versions include "I slit a sheet, a sheet I slit" and "I slit a sheet, a sheet I slit and on the slitted sheet I sit." There is even "I slit two sheets, two sheets I slit. Now I sit on the slitted sheet." The misarticulation of this tongue twister obviously results in the utterance of a taboo word.

I mentioned earlier that the variation may be limited to a single word or a single sentence. Let me give an example of the latter. In an overtly sexist joke, a man decides he wants to become a woman and so he goes to Denmark to have a sex-change operation performed. When he returns, three of his old friends go out with him to a bar. The first asks, "Did it hurt when the doctors removed your male organ?" "Oh, no, there was a total anesthetic. I didn't feel a thing." The second inquires, "Did it hurt when they constructed a female anatomical part in its place?" "Oh, no, as I told you, there was a total anesthetic. I didn't feel any pain." The third then wonders, "Did anything about the whole process cause you any distress at all?" "Oh, yes, when they put a straw in my ear and sucked out half my brain." Now this very same joke can be told verbatim with just the last line changed. In response to the third friend's query, we have instead, "Oh, yes, when I went back to work and received only half my pay." What a difference one sentence can make! But that is precisely the reason folklorists are so adamant about the importance of collecting as many versions of an item of folklore as possible. There is always a risk of misinterpretation if one has only one version. In this way, the study of folklore differs markedly from the study of literature, as there is usually only a single text of a poem or short story.

Multiple existence and variation are characteristic of all genres of folklore: proverbs, jokes, legends, and so on. There is a contemporary legend about a woman with a pet poodle. She gives it a bath, but then afterwards she is worried that it will catch cold, so she decides to pop it in her microwave oven to dry it off quickly. The microwave explodes, killing her beloved pet. Exactly the same legend (typically told as a true occurrence, a particular characteristic of the legend genre, as opposed to folktales told as fiction) is related, but with a cat instead of a poodle. The point is that the variation may be minimal, but if an item is authentic folklore, there is bound to be variation of some kind. In the exploding microwave legend, by the way, we once again have an example of antiwoman folklore. Poodle or cat, it is almost always a woman who is depicted as unable to understand the nature of such modern technology as a microwave oven.

One last modern legend may help to show the range of variation in one particular story. Rather than presenting different versions, I shall give a composite account. One or two white women are alone in an elevator in a posh hotel in New York or Los Angeles or Las Vegas. Suddenly, the door opens and a black man enters, sometimes alone, sometimes with one or two companions. In all versions, he has a large dog with him, sometimes on a leash. The man says (to the dog), "Sit, Lady" or in other versions, "Sit, bitch" or "Sit, Whitey" (the dog is white-colored). In one variant, he instructs his companion to "Hit the floor" (meaning to push the elevator button for their destination). In all versions, the woman or women immediately drop to the floor of the elevator in fear. (In the Las Vegas versions, the women are carrying buckets of coins won from the slot machines, and when they drop to the floor the buckets spill, making a terrible clatter.) The black man says nothing, but the next morning when the woman or women go to check out of the hotel, they find their bill has been paid. There may be a note attached, often with flowers, saying "Thanks for the laugh" or "That's the best laugh I've had in years," signed Reggie Jackson (the baseball player) or Eddie Murphy (the movie star) or some other African American celebrity. This "elevator incident" legend is very revealing about the irrational fears of white women (and their ignorance—they presumably should have been able to recognize the celebrity in question). It also signals the magnanimity of the celebrity, who refuses to take offense at the racist insult and returns the affront with kindness and generosity. Of course, "killing with kindness" may constitute a means of humiliating the paranoid white women to punish them for their racist prejudice. This technique of being overly kind to offenders is reminiscent of the passage in Romans: "*If thine enemy hunger, feed him; if he thirst, give him drink: for in so doing thou shalt heap coals of fire on his head*" (Rom. 12:20). The point here, however, is once again to demonstrate a remarkable degree of variation, for example, what the black man said, the number of women or men, and the identity of the celebrity. The variation found in this legend is by no means atypical. Variation is the very hallmark of folklore.

Written Folklore

Assuming that it is now understood that the defining criteria of folklore include multiple existence and variation, we can imagine that a skeptic might question the relevance of all this to the Bible. The examples of folklore cited thus far—proverbs, jokes, and legends—are all **orally** transmitted. The Bible is a **written** document. Why then would we expect multiple existence and variation to be a factor in understanding the Bible? There are two answers to this question. First, the Bible was originally in oral tradition. That is the case with both the Old and New Testaments, so the rules or principles of oral tradition may well apply. Second, oral transmission is a common but not absolutely essential factor in defining folklore. There is written folklore as well as oral folklore. Moreover, the same criteria that apply to oral folklore are also applicable to written folklore. We may briefly consider several examples of written folklore to illustrate this.

Let us start with flyleaf inscriptions, the short poems placed on the inside cover of books, especially schoolbooks.

> Marlboro is my dwelling place,
> America's my nation,
> Henry Dudley is my name,
> And Christ is my salvation.

An alternative last line is "And heaven my expectation."

> Mary Johnson is my name,
> Ireland is my nation,

Clady More's my dwelling-place,
And heaven my expectation.

Note that the sequence of the lines varies. The name of the writer is in the third line of the first version but in the first line of the second. Such sequential variation is common in folklore, both oral and written. This same poem is also found in autograph book verse:

Mary is my name.
Grandville is my station.
I sit in school all day and fool
And that's my education.

A more common autograph book or friendship book variant is:

Gloria is your name,
Single is your station.
Happy is the lucky man
Who makes the alteration.

It is a simple enough matter to demonstrate the variation in such written folklore as autograph book verse. Consider the following three versions of a rather sentimental example:

When **nature** folds her curtains back
And pins them with a star,
Remember that you have a friend
Although she wanders far.

When **time** pulls back its curtains
And pins them with a star,
Remember you have a friend
No matter where you are.

When **night** has pulled her curtain
And pinned it with a star,
Remember you have a friend
Wherever you are.

One last example of autograph book verse should suffice:

Down in a **valley**
On a modest little spot
Grows a little flower
Called forget-me-not.

Down by the **river,**
Carved on a rock;
Are these words
"Forget me not."

Way out in the **ocean**
Carved on a rock
Are **three** little words
Forget-me-not.

Down in the **cellar**
Carved on a rock
Are **four** little words
For-get-me-not.

The same principles are also manifested in other forms of written folk-lore, such as graffiti or a subset of that category, namely, bathroom wall writings, or latrinalia:

You can wiggle, jiggle, jump or dance
But the last **three** drops go down your pants.

No matter how you dance and prance
The last **two** drops go down your pants.

Folklore, whether oral or written, is characterized by multiple existence and variation. The variation may be reflected in such details as different names, different numbers, or different sequences of lines.

Perhaps the most striking example of written folklore is what has been termed photocopier or xerographic. This form of folklore is also to be found transmitted by fax, E-mail, and the Internet. There are hundreds of examples of this type of folklore. I shall present just two versions of one item to illustrate the genre:

Governmental Economics 101

Socialism is when you have two cows and you give one to your neighbor.

Communism is when you have two cows and the government takes both of them and gives you the milk.

...cism is when you have two cows and the government takes both of them and sells you the milk.

Nazism is when you have two cows and the government takes both of them and shoots you.

Capitalism is when you have two cows and you sell one to buy a bull.

Bureaucracy is when you have two cows, the state takes both of them, shoots one, milks the other, and throws the milk away.

The Intelligent Human's Guide to Cows and Politics

SOCIALISM
You have two cows. Give one to your neighbor.

COMMUNISM
You have two cows. Give them both to the government. Government gives you milk.

FASCISM
You have two cows. Give milk to government. Government sells it.

NAZISM
Government shoots you and takes cows.

NEW DEALISM
Government shoots one cow, milks the other, and pours milk down the sink.

CAPITALISM
Sell one cow. Buy bull.

ANARCHISM
Keep cows. Shoot government. Steal another cow.

CONSERVATISM
Embalm cows. Freeze milk.

LIBERALISM
Give milk back to cows. Let them escape.

So the list of folklore genres includes not only orally transmitted ones such as myths, folktales, legends, proverbs, riddles, superstitions, curses, charms, tongue twisters, and games, but also written ones such as autograph book verses, chain letters, graffiti, and photocopier or fax folklore.

Previous Studies of Folklore and the Bible

The recognition of written folklore is critical to our consideration of the Bible. It is precisely the failure of all previous biblical scholars to recognize this that tends to invalidate all earlier research. By equating folklore with oral tradition only, these scholars supposedly were able to distinguish between folklore (oral tradition) on the one hand and the Bible (written tradition) on the other. Once the oral criterion is removed or shown to be inadequate, the supposed distinction between oral folklore and the written Bible is placed in serious doubt. But even the oral element was not properly understood. It is not enough to acknowledge that the Bible was in oral tradition before being written down with the assumption that once written down, folklore ceases to be folklore. But, strange to say, this is what is stated in the scholarship: *"a tradition ceases to be such at that point at which it is removed . . . from its normal context in life and is entered into a written composition"* (Knight 1975:27; emphasis in original). This is a faulty premise. An oral proverb once written down does not then magically cease to be a proverb. Once a proverb, always a proverb! A legend once written down does not stop being a legend. The point is that if the Bible was once folklore, why is it not still folklore? Just because it was written down does not automatically negate its original folkloristic nature.

It is also worth observing that the original oral tradition does not disappear once folklore is recorded in writing. A singer of a folk song does not stop singing that folk song after a folklorist records the song. The folk song more often than not continues to be sung and transmitted from person to person and from generation to generation. Non-folklorists, including Bible scholars, tend to underestimate the tremendous tenacity of tradition. Let me give an example. A papyrus palimpsest recovered from Elephantine in Upper Egypt in the first decade of the twentieth century contained an Aramaic text of the story of Ahiqar dating from the late fifth century b.c. It is, in fact, a traditional tale, namely, Aarne-Thompson tale type 922A, *Achikar,* in which a falsely accused minister reinstates himself by his cleverness. This folktale has been the subject of countless monographs (Aarne and Thompson 1961). The wisdom of the protagonist is demonstrated by his citation of numerous proverbs. One of the proverbs of Ahiqar is:

> Do not be too sweet lest you be swallowed;
> Do not be too bitter lest you be spat out (Lindenberger 1983:149; cf.
> Pritchard 1950:429).

In 1937, an essay published in the *Revue des Études Islamiques* included a proverb elicited from a Kurdish informant who was an emir's servant:

> *Do not be too sweet, they will eat you,*
> *Do not be too bitter, they will vomit you* (Lescot 1937:344).

Both of these versions of the same proverb come from the same general area of the Middle East, but they are separated by more than two thousand years. There is also a version reported in an Arabic manuscript, Muhammad Al-Shahrastáni's *Book of Religious and Philosophical Sects*, compiled in 1127, a version that has been translated as:

> *My son, do not be too sweet, lest they swallow thee,*
> *and do not be too bitter, lest they vomit thee out* (Lindenberger 1983:263).

The proverb is not, however, confined to the Middle East. There is also a Sicilian version: "*Not so sweet that every one will suck you, nor so bitter that everyone will spit you out,*" as well as a Serbian variant: "*Be neither honey, lest men lick thee up, nor poison, lest they spit thee out*" (Crane 1885:312). In 1920, a published book on life in India reported that a mother's advice to her daughter included the following:

> *Do not be as sweet as sugar, or they will overwhelm you with work, nor as sour as a nim leaf, or they will spit you out* (Stevenson 1920:106).

The advice referred to the common plight of a child-wife forced to survive in a household of strange and often nagging women, including her mother-in-law.

This is by no means an atypical example of the remarkable tenacity of tradition. Orally transmitted folklore such as proverbs and legends can survive relatively intact for centuries with no help from written sources. In modern times, we tend to rely heavily upon print or other means of recording data, and we fail to realize that humankind throughout most of its collective history has depended almost exclusively upon orally transmitted knowledge.

There are two additional issues I wish to raise before turning to our consideration of the Bible. The first matter again has to do with the term "folklore." To identify or label a verbal account as folklore says nothing one way or the other as to the historicity of that account. Some folklore is historically accurate; some is not. Each instance has to be examined on an individual basis. The existence of legends told about George Washington surely does not prove that George Washington never existed. Perhaps he did not actually chop down his father's beloved cherry tree—this is what historians claim. But from a folkloristic perspective, this legend of Washington is not without significance. Probably the best-known story about Washington, the legend does reveal something about the folk attitude toward presidents in general and Washington in particular. It reports a father-son confrontation (as England versus its "son" colony America) and suggests that Americans might tend to see the president as a rebellious son who eventually becomes a glorified father figure. Another repeated local legend to the effect that "George Washington **slept** here," not to mention the particular monument erected by a grateful citizenry, further confirms the Oedipal constellation involving the "father" of our country. In true folkloristic fashion, the rising "son" has to cut down the tree of his father, analogous to young King Arthur removing his father's sword stuck in the maternal stone scabbard, or in modern popular culture to Luke Skywalker learning how to handle his father's extraordinary light saber (which is magically extensible and contains the "life force"). In the case of George Washington and the cherry tree legend, historians notwithstanding, what the folk **think** happened or **say** happened might be just as important as what **actually** happened. For an entree into the considerable scholarship devoted to determining whether oral tradition can be considered a valid source of authentic historical data, see Jan Vansina's *Oral Tradition as History* (1985), folklorist Richard M. Dorson's survey "The Debate over the Trustworthiness of Oral Traditional History" (1972), and Robert C. Culley's "Oral Tradition and Historicity" (1972). For representative discussions focused on the Middle East or the Bible, see Eduard Nielsen's *Oral Tradition* (1954), Dov Zlotnick's "Memory and the Integrity of the Oral Tradition" (1984–85), and Kenneth E. Bailey's "Informal Controlled Tradition and the Synoptic Gospels" (1991).

The second issue concerns the term "oral literature." I do not like this term at all. It is an obvious oxymoron. "Literature" refers to something written, so how can there be such a thing as "oral" literature? The term is used by elitist literary scholars who are uncomfortable with the term "folklore" and who are trying to upgrade the material by calling it "literature." The fallacy of the concept is easily demonstrated once one realizes that from an evolutionary point of view, oral tradition has everywhere preceded a written language. Oral tradition or folklore has its own identity, totally independent of writing. There can be no question that peoples told tales for centuries before written forms of language came into being. Why then do I employ the term "oral literature" here?

The reason is that the Bible, in my view, is orally based, but it is obviously a written document. Hence it makes some sense to call the Bible oral literature. It is codified oral tradition, or codified folklore. Moreover, there is precedent in biblical scholarship for this point of view. R. C. Culley, in "An Approach to the Problem of Oral Tradition," puts the matter this way: "The term 'oral literature' is, of course, a contradiction, as is the term 'unwritten literature.' Literature suggests something written. Nevertheless, the term 'oral literature' is used by many and will be retained here. Oral literature is merely literature which has come into existence in an oral culture or group without the use of writing. Sometimes such literature is called folklore" (1963:118).

It has long been recognized that there was a connection between folklore and the Bible (but not that the Bible **was** folklore!). Some scholars, recognizing the fact that both the Old and New Testaments were orally transmitted before being recorded in written form, became particularly interested in folklorists' studies of oral tradition. The logic was that if one could identify the laws of oral transmission, that is, what happens to an item of folklore as it is transmitted from person to person and from generation to generation, then one could in theory work in reverse to establish the "true" elements of the Bible. In other words, if the Bible is the product or end result of the oral transmission process, then by seeking to reverse the mostly negative effects of that process—the German term for this allegedly destructive process in folk song is *zersingen*—then one could peel off the errors that had crept in and reconstruct the original (read "historically bona fide") facts.

Another group of scholars sought to identify folklore **in** the Bible. A classic example of this approach is James George Frazer's *Folklore in the Old Testament*. Frazer (1854–1941) was a classicist and comparativist. His method consisted of ransacking the world's ethnographic and folkloristic literature in search of apparent parallels to items in the Old Testament. He cited nearly two hundred pages of parallels to the flood myth, for example. Although Frazer tended to favor polygenesis rather than monogenesis and diffusion as an explanation of parallel texts, the existence of many versions of the flood myth did not necessarily argue against the historicity of the event. Quite the contrary. The hundreds of versions of the flood myth could presumably be presented as evidence that a catastrophic deluge did occur.

Another pioneering figure in the study of folklore and the Bible was Hermann Gunkel (1862–1932). Gunkel was one of the founders of an approach to the Bible known as Form Criticism, one goal of which was to reconstruct the oral state that immediately preceded the written Bible (Tucker 1971:9). Two of his most important contributions were *Genesis übersetzt und erklärt* (1901), translated into English as *The Legends of Genesis* (1964), and *Das Märchen im Alten Testament* (1921), translated into English as *The Folktale in the Old Testament* (1987). In attempting to disentangle history from what he termed "legend," Gunkel argued that legend came from oral tradition as opposed to "history proper," which "is usually found in written form" (1964:3). Gunkel insisted, "There is no denying that there are legends in the Old Testament" (1964:3). Gunkel's task, as he saw it, was to evaluate the content of Genesis in that context. "Now it is evident," argued Gunkel, "that Genesis contains the final sublimation into writing of a body of oral traditions," and he commented on the "parallel" issue by saying, "Now we cannot regard the story of the Deluge in Genesis as history and that of the Babylonians as legend" (1964:4, 10). Gunkel believed that the "legends" of Genesis were "faded myths" (1964:143). A modern folklorist would not accept Gunkel's distinction. There are a number of myths in Genesis: the creation of humankind and the flood myth, to mention just two. A myth is defined as a "sacred narrative explaining how the world and mankind came to be in their present form" (Dundes 1984). So there are myths in the Bible (cf. Ohler 1969; Otzen, Gottlieb, and Jeppesen 1980) as well as many other folklore genres such as folktales, legends, proverbs, and curses. No folklorist would accept anthropologist Edmund Leach's sweeping generalization that "the whole of the Bible is myth for Christians and the whole of the Old Testament is myth for Jews" (Leach 1983:8). (For a useful summary of Gunkel's approach to folklore and the Bible, see Gibert 1979; Kirkpatrick 1988:223–34.)

Still another interesting effort to study the relationship between folklore and the Bible was that of French folklorist Emile Nourry (1870–1935), writing under the pseudonym P. Saintyves. Perhaps the most important of this prolific writer's many contributions to the subject was *Essais de Folklore Biblique: Magie, Mythes et Miracles dans l'Ancien et le Nouveau Testament* (1922). Saintyves, a myth-ritualist, fell more into Frazer's camp than Gunkel's. The book, however, represents a departure from Frazer, who considered only the Old Testament. Saintyves's nine essays refer to both the Old and the New Testaments, for example, essays on Aaron's Rod and the circumambulatory destruction of the walls of Jericho as well as the miracles of changing water into wine and multiplying loaves of bread.

There are many other scholarly investigations of folklore and the Bible, including Thorlief Boman, *Die Jesus-Überlieferung im Lichte der neueren Volkskunde* (1967), J. W. Rogerson, *Myth in Old Testament Interpretation* (1974), Albert B. Lord,"The Gospels as Oral Traditional Literature" (1978), Pamela J. Milne, *Vladimir Propp and the Study of Structure in Hebrew Biblical Narrative* (1988), Patricia G. Kirkpatrick, *The Old Testament and Folklore Study* (1988), Robert C. Culley, *Studies in the Structure of Hebrew Narrative* (1976b) and *Themes and Variations* (1992), Susan Niditch, *Underdogs and Tricksters: A Prelude to Biblical Folklore* (1987), *Folklore and the Hebrew Bible* (1993), and *Oral World and Written Word: Ancient Israelite Literature* (1996). It is certainly not my intention to provide an in-depth survey of all previous scholarship involving folklore and the Bible. That would be an enormous task worthy of a doctoral dissertation. My general impression, however, is that almost all earlier scholarship tends to be partial and piecemeal. Either it treats one particular theme or passage or it is limited to just the Old or the New Testament.

In the absence of a full-scale review of all previous scholarship on folklore and the Bible, I am obliged to acknowledge that there are numerous statements recognizing the oral priority of Biblical traditions, and this is true of both Old Testament and New Testament researchers.

Ivan Engnell wrote, "But it is . . . important to appreciate . . . the function, extensiveness, and significance of the oral traditional stage. It is only when we assume that much of the material now in the Pentateuch was handed down orally at an early stage that we can explain the problem of variants in the Pentateuch, because such variants are particularly typical of literature which has been transmitted orally" (Engnell 1970:53–54). The same Swedish scholar who was a strong advocate of the necessity of taking "oral tradition" into account in studying the Old Testament (cf. Anderson 1950; Willis 1970:391–92) listed "the doublet and variant system" as the very first of the criteria to be used to judge "the oral form of tradition" (Engnell 1960:24). (For a detailed discussion of Engnell and many other Scandinavian scholars who debated various degrees of the importance of taking oral tradition into account in studying the Bible, see Knight 1975:217–399.) "Since the four canonical Gospels were written between 35 and 70 years after the crucifixion, one must have some theory of 'oral tradition' to write a history of Jesus. That an extensive tradition existed behind the Gospels has been taken for granted" (Henaut 1993:15). Martin Dibelius (1936:35) put the matter this way:

> the narrative sections of the Gospels are not at all concerned with giving a chronicle of events, with biography, or with making a connected historical record. What is set down is essentially stories in narrative form, complete in themselves. In form at least they are similar to our anecdotes, and they deal with separate incidents in the life of Jesus. They would not have come down to us rounded off and complete in themselves . . . if they had not been current separately in the first instance, passed on from mouth to mouth independently of each other.

Moreover, as Klaus Koch observes, the "period of written transmission until its final, canonical form is sometimes quite short in comparison with the previous long span of oral tradition" (1969:77). This was especially true in the case of the Old Testament. "Nearly all the Old Testament, whether the Tetrateuch stories, the psalms, or prophetic speeches, had been passed down orally for a long period before they came to be written down" (Koch 1969:81). In this context, it seems reasonable to regard both the Old and New Testaments as written down "codified oral tradition" (Widengren 1959:212). As one perceptive scholar phrased it, "Mark's taking up the pen is therefore not a real act of composition but a variant of the oral. . . ." (Güttegemanns 1979:138).

Rudolf Bultmann, a leading biblical scholar of the twentieth century, clearly acknowledged the presence and role of oral tradition. For him, it was "a matter of indifference whether the tradition were oral or written, because on account of the unliterary character of the material one of the chief differences between oral and written traditions is lacking" (1963:6). He claimed that "There is no definable boundary between the oral and written tradition" and that the question of whether formulations of the New Testament Gospels took place in an oral or written stage of tradition was "relatively unimportant. Both stages of the tradition need to be taken into account" (1963:321, 348). This is similar to Engnell's statement that "oral tradition and transmission in writing should not be played off as mutually exclusive alternatives, but be considered as methods, *running alongside and complementing each other*" (1960:23, emphasis in original). This view is further expressed as "if we are bidden to choose between oral tradition and writing we must decline the either-or and insist on having both" (North 1954–55:39). The apostle Paul recognized the importance of both the oral word and the written epistle in his efforts to proselytize prospective Christians: "*Therefore, brethren, stand fast, and hold the traditions which ye have been taught, **whether by word, or our epistle**" (2 Thess. 2:15).

There is another critical point with respect to the coexistence of oral and written traditions. As Solomon Gandz observes in his neglected 1935 essay "Oral Tradition in the Bible," the innovation of writing did not obviate the need for oral tradition. Quite the contrary. He argues that writing down sacred texts was originally strictly a mnemonic aid designed to facilitate the accurate **oral** transmission of those texts (Gandz 1935:254, cf. Neusner 1987). A written text made it easier to teach others—the majority of whom probably could not read anyway—to memorize or learn by heart texts deemed important. This process is well described in Deuteronomy 31. First God instructs Moses as follows: "*Now therefore write ye this song for you, and teach it the children of Israel: put it in their mouths, that this song may be a witness for me. . . . And it shall come to pass, when many evils and troubles are befallen them, that this song shall testify against them as a witness; for it shall not be forgotten out of the mouths of their seed. . . . Moses therefore **wrote** this song the same day, and taught it the children of Israel*" (Deut. 31:19, 21, 22). The oral teaching by Moses is made even more explicit: "*Gather unto me all the elders of your tribes, and your officers, that I may **speak** these words in their ears, and call heaven and earth to record against them. . . . And Moses **spake** in the ears of all the congregation of Israel the words of this song, until they were ended*" (Deut. 31:28, 30). And the initial words of the song confirm its oral nature: "*Give ear, O ye heavens, and I will speak; and hear, O earth, the words of my mouth*" (Deut. 32:1). In modern times, some missionaries have recognized the utility of teaching the Bible orally, especially among peoples who cannot read or write (Klem 1982).

In biblical times, members of the congregation were expected to commit songs and other texts to memory by reciting them over and over until they were completely memorized. Learning by rote could be accomplished almost anywhere. God makes this clear to Moses: "*And these words, which I commanded thee this day, shall be in thine heart: And thou shalt teach them diligently unto thy children, and shall talk of them when thou sittest in thine house, and when thou walkest by the way, and when thou liest down, and when thou risest up"* (Deut. 6:6–7). Much the same sentiment is expressed by Deborah when she sings her song of praise to God: *"Speak, ye that ride on white asses, ye that sit in judgment, and walk by the way. They that are delivered from the noise of archers in the places of drawing water, there shall they rehearse the righteous acts of the Lord"* (Judg. 5:10–11). Whether one is engaged in riding, walking, or sitting, one can utilize the time to recite a text in order to learn it by heart.

The very last book of the Old Testament provides a strong reminder that (1) knowledge comes from oral tradition—therefore not from written texts—and that (2) priests who do not learn texts by heart will be punished by God:

> *For the priest's lips should keep knowledge, and they should seek the law at his mouth: for he is the messenger of the Lord of hosts* (Mal. 2:7).

> *And now, O ye priests, this commandment is for you. If he will not hear, and if he will not lay it to heart, to give glory unto my name, saith the Lord of hosts. I will even send a curse upon you, and I will curse your blessings: yea, I have cursed them already, because ye do not lay it to heart. Beyond, I will corrupt your seed, and spread dung upon your faces, even the dung of your solemn feasts; and one shall take you away with it* (Mal. 21:1–3).

These passages come from the Old Testament, but much the same attitudes apply to the New Testament as well. It may be difficult for modern readers so accustomed to the authority of the written word to appreciate the earlier relationship between oral and written tradition. As Gandz (1935:261) astutely remarked, in biblical times written documents were of lesser importance and had to be confirmed by oral testimonies. In this regard, we may note that Papias of Hierapolis in Phrygia writing early in the second century—as reported by Eusebius of Caesarea in his classic of the early fourth century *History of the Church*—appeared to favor oral over written tradition: "For I did not imagine that things out of books would help me as much as the utterances of a living and abiding voice" (Eusebius 1965:102; for the view that this suggests only that eyewitnesses are more reliable sources than nonwitnesses' written accounts and not the superiority of oral over written transmission, see Hanson 1962:38). This belief in the primacy of oral tradition is in marked contrast to modern times, when oral tradition is deemed untrustworthy and must be confirmed by written documents ("Get it in writing"), and this is also true in the case of the New Testament.

Albert Lord, who did have a theory of oral tradition, wrote an essay entitled "The Gospels as Oral Traditional Literature." Lord (1978:5) erred in labeling the Gospels "myths," a genre mistake almost as misguided as considering them folktales: "If the Gospels are a story, orally conditioned, then we may legitimately call them a folktale" (Brewer 1979:39). Folktales, of course, by definition are **fiction** as opposed to history or truth. The Gospels are clearly legends, not myths, if one accepts the definition of myth as a sacred narrative explaining how the world and humankind came to be in their present form, whereas a legend is a narrative told as true set in the postcreation world. However, Lord does rightly conclude, "There is enough . . . evidence to indicate that these gospels are closely related to oral traditional literature" (1978:90–91). Part of the evidence adduced by Lord is his noting "several instances of duplication of multiforms. This is peculiarly an oral traditional phenomenon" (1978:90).

The history of the relationship of oral tradition to the Bible has been well documented, and the interested reader should refer to such sources as Boman (1967), Güttegemanns (1979), Culley (1986), Kirkpatrick (1988), and especially Niditch (1987, 1990, 1996), arguably the leading scholar in this area. Among the long list of discussions of this relationship are Lods 1923, Gandz 1935, Hempel 1938, Van der Ploeg 1947, North 1949–50, Ringgren 1950–51, Doeve 1957, Stuhmueller 1958, Widengren 1959, Ahlström 1966, Hahn 1987, and Aranda 1997, to mention a few.

In light of my insistence upon "multiple existence" and "variation" as the two most salient characteristics of folklore, I wish to emphasize Engnell's remark that variants are a feature of oral tradition and Lord's similar comment that the "duplication of multiforms" is "peculiarly an oral traditional phenomenon." The suggestion that "doublets" were a telltale sign of oral tradition is an old one. Johann Gottfried Herder, one of the founders of folkloristics and the creator of the term "Volkslied" (folk song) in 1773, saw the existence of "double traditions" as an indication of oral traditional elements in the Bible (Willi 1971:64, Knight 1975:59). A few scholars have questioned whether doublets are necessarily prima facie evidence of orality, arguing that writers might use repetition as a means of emphasis (Knight 1975:238 n. 12, 314 n. 34, 375 n. 35). But from a folkloristic perspective, there can be no doubt whatsoever that doublets and triple repetitions demonstrate a likely oral origin. Yet not everyone understands the nature of multiple existence and variation as criteria of oral tradition that so often result in doublets and even texts repeated three or more times. Consider the following misinformed question: "If a *fixed* oral tradition is the source behind all four canonical gospels, why is there so much variation among them?" (Teeple 1970:60). The same author in his essay entitled "The Oral Tradition That Never Existed" actually uses the high incidence of variation as an argument against the existence of an oral tradition underlying the New Testament: "Further evidence against the theory of an authentic oral tradition is the tremendous variety in the early Christian literature. If such an oral tradition was circulating throughout the Christian communities, why is there so much diversity and sometimes inconsistency in the beliefs and writings of the early Christians?" (Teeple 1970:65). The point is that oral tradition by its very nature has variation as one of its principal defining characteristics. Far from arguing **against** prior oral tradition, variation clearly argues **for** the preexistence of oral tradition.

Although it is true that many scholars have acknowledged that both the Old and New Testaments were originally in oral tradition before being written down, they have, in my opinion, failed to carry that admission to its logical conclusion. In effect, the nod to prior oral tradition consists largely of lip service. Yes, there was initial oral tradition, but then these scholars go on to consider the Bible as a purely religious or literary text, totally ignoring the possible debt to oral tradition. For the vast majority of Bible scholars, "Oral tradition is an uncertain and usually corruptible vehicle of information," and "In situations where both written and oral tradition exist, written tradition drives out oral" (Hanson 1962:17, 21). This literary bias or "bookish" penchant has plagued folklorists too. The Grimm brothers and other nineteenth-century collectors could not refrain from "improving" their oral texts by rewriting them. In the twentieth century, too many folklorists made the mistake of interpreting folklore using "literary" criteria. Forcing folklore to conform to literary standards and interpreting folklore as if it were written literature are both results of a long-standing failure to accept folklore on its own terms and judging it as such. Even Susan Niditch, who devoted an entire book to criticizing the neglect of prior oral tradition by Biblical scholars, in the end succumbs to the inevitable literary bias: "Rather than think of the Bible as a book," she says, "we do well to think of the Bible as a library" (1996:116). And in fairness, it should be kept in mind that the very word "bible" comes from the word for book. It is derived from the same root that yields the French *bibliothéque* (library) and the English "bibliography" and "bibliophile." The same bias is reflected in the common designation of "The Good Book" as **Scripture**. The word "scripture," of course, comes from a root meaning "writing." Nevertheless, I maintain the Bible consists of **orally transmitted tradition written down.** Certainly there were collations, "literary" emendations, and editorial tampering, but the folkloristic component of the Bible remains in plain sight even if blind scholars have failed to recognize it as such.

Calling scholars "blind" may be too harsh a judgment. From a historical perspective, it is not hard to discover why students of the Bible might not want to recognize or acknowledge its folkloristic nature. It turns out that studying the content of the Bible could prove to be a risky proposition, definitely dangerous to one's health or professional standing. A French Catholic priest, Richard Simon (1638–1712) published his path-breaking *Histoire critique du Vieux Testament* in 1678, in which he disputed the single authorship of the Pentateuch. One of the criteria for his argument was the obvious repetition of diverse descriptions of the same incident (Knight 1975:47). The book's publication resulted in Simon's dismissal from his clerical position and his book's being suppressed and in fact officially placed on the Catholic *Index librorum prohibitorum* in 1683 (Knight 1975:45). This sort of scenario has occurred many times. In 1835 David Friedrich Strauss published his important *Leben Jesu*. Using a modified form of the comparative method, Strauss considered the four Gospels as variants and sought to isolate contradictory elements in an attempt to separate what he regarded as "mythus" from history. This book cost Strauss his teaching position and his academic career (Dundes 1980:227). Similarly, Ernest Renan (1823–92), author of *Vie de Jésus* (1863) was forced to resign his chair of Hebrew and Chaldaic Languages at the Collège de France because of his unorthodox views. William Robertson Smith (1846–94), after being educated at Aberdeen University, enrolled in 1866 as a student of theology at the Free Church college in Edinburgh. In 1870, he became professor of Oriental languages and Old Testament exegesis at the same institution. However, articles on Biblical matters that he contributed to the ninth edition of the *Encyclopaedia Britannica* upset the authorities at the college, who rebuked him. Smith requested a formal trial at which he defended himself ably. Nevertheless, he failed to get a necessary vote of confidence, and in 1881 he was officially removed from his chair. In this case, Smith managed to survive his dismissal, going on to a professorship at Cambridge in 1883 and writing, among other influential works, *Lectures on the Religion of the Semites* in 1889. But the overall message is crystal-clear and bound to give pause to anyone thinking of subjecting the Bible to any kind of new critical examination.

Variation in Number, Name, and Sequence

It is time now to turn to the Bible and show its folkloristic nature. There are hundreds of possible illustrations of multiple existence and variation, so many in fact that it is difficult to know which ones to choose. I hope to show that virtually every major event in both the Old and New Testaments exist in at least two versions.

Let us begin with a relatively simple example. Consider this passage in Matthew 10:29–31:

> *Are there not **two sparrows sold for a farthing?** And one of them shall not fall on the ground without your Father. But the very hairs of your head are all numbered. Fear ye not therefore, ye are of more value than many sparrows.*

We may compare this with Luke 12:6–7:

> *Are not five sparrows sold for two farthings and not one of them is forgotten before God? But even the very hairs of your head are all numbered. Fear not therefore: ye are of more value than many sparrows.*

Assuming Jesus used this sparrow metaphor, presumably he spoke of either *"two sparrows sold for a farthing"* or *"five sparrows sold for two farthings."* Perhaps this is a trivial example, but one could easily multiply such examples a hundredfold in the Bible. What we clearly have here are two versions of the same incident, and they are versions with some variation. In short, we have an example of folklore!

Variation in Number

Variation in number is a common feature of multiple existence. We may see another striking example in two distinct versions of the flood myth. These two versions are recounted as a purported single narrative in Genesis 6–8, but the compiler(s) did not bother to iron out the obvious inconsistencies in the two versions, and that is fortunate for us, as it allows us to distinguish some of the salient differential elements. I shall confine my comparison to just three details, two of which involve numbers.

The first concerns the number of animals Noah is instructed to bring aboard the famous ark.

> *And of every living thing of all flesh,* **two** *of every sort shalt thou bring into the ark, to keep them alive with thee; they shall be male and female. Of fowls after their kind, and of cattle after their kind, of every creeping thing of the earth after his kind;* **two** *of every sort shall come unto thee, to keep them alive* (Gen. 6:19–20).

> *Of every clean beast thou shalt take to thee by* **sevens,** *the male and his female: and of beasts that are not clean by two, the male and his female. Of fowls also of the air by* **sevens,** *the male and the female: to keep seed alive upon the face of the earth* (Gen. 7:2–3).

The second numerical detail has to do with the alleged duration of the flood.

> *And the waters returned from off the earth continually: and after the end of the* **hundred and fifty days** *the waters were abated* (Gen. 8:3).

> *And it came to pass at the end of* **forty days,** *that Noah opened the window of the ark which he had made* (Gen. 8:6).

Forty is the traditional ritual number of the Middle East signifying "a lot of." That is why the children of Israel were obliged to wander in the wilderness for forty years (Numbers 14:33, 32:13; Deuteronomy 8:2). This why the children of Israel ate manna for forty years (Exodus 16:35). That is why Jesus *"was there in the wilderness forty days tempted of Satan"* (Mark 1:13) and why Jesus *"fasted forty days and forty nights"* (Matt. 4:2). This also explains the extraordinary coincidence that King David and son Solomon, his successor, **both** just happened to rule for a period of forty years (2 Samuel 5:4; 1 Kings 2:11; 1 Chronicles 29:27; 1 Kings 11:42; 2 Chronicles 9:30). The number forty remains traditional two thousand years later, as in the Arabic tale of "Ali Baba and the Forty Thieves" and in contemporary Jewish folklore, which includes a wish that an individual might live 'til one hundred and twenty," the product of the ritual number three and the number forty. (For a further discussion of the significance of the number forty in the Middle East, see Brandes 1985:57–59, 68–72.)

A third detail in the two versions of the flood myth is not a numerical one. Rather it concerns the particular bird that Noah sent forth to ascertain if the flood waters had receded enough to allow the ark's passengers to disembark safely.

*And he sent forth a **raven** which went forth to and fro, until the waters were dried up from off the earth* (Gen. 8:7).

*He sent forth a **dove** from him to see if the waters were abated from off the face of the ground* (Gen. 8:8).

In this brief consideration of the flood myth, we can see that the versions differ with respect to the numbers of animals taken on board the ark, the number of days it took for the flood to abate, and the type of bird Noah sent out to determine whether it was safe to leave the ark. (For a further comparison of two different versions of the flood myth in Genesis, see Habel 1971:29–42; for the flood myth in general, see Dundes 1988.) It should be noted that most of the Bible scholars who have noticed these and similar discrepancies have been primarily concerned with identifying the various voices or authors in the Old Testament. These voices or authors are conventionally designated by letters derived from the particular lexical choice for the name of God. Thus J stands for the individual who used Jehovah or Yahweh, E for the individual who preferred Elohim, D for the author of Deuteronomy, and P for the so-called priestly writer, among others. The search for such sources is certainly a legitimate one, but scholars engaged in such a search tend to be biased in favor of literature and against oral tradition. The idea that the Old Testament is a combination of different sources is known as the "Documentary Hypothesis" (Friedman 1989:26), and the assumption is that the sources were **written documents** rather than oral tradition. Friedman's fascinating book seeking to pin down the identity of the compilers of these sources is entitled *Who **Wrote** the Bible?* (my emphasis). Here is a representative statement: "Was P an old set of stories, told orally for a long time, that the P writer merely collected and set down? Some biblical scholars believe that much of the Bible was originally oral composition. I see no evidence at all for this in the case of P" (Friedman 1989:215). I have no wish to enter into a debate over the possible oral components of P. But I should point out that the same bias with respect to identifying authorial strands in the Old Testament is also found in New Testament scholarship. So there has been much ink spilled in discussions of who Matthew, Mark, Luke, and John were. The goals are to date the various strands, evaluate their historicity, and determine degrees of intertextuality. Bultmann, for example, claims (1963:1, 6, 338, 353–54, 362) that Mark's gospel is the earliest and that both Matthew and Luke drew on Mark but added elements from another source (for which we do not have a text, but a hypothetical reconstruction of which from Matthew and Luke is referred to in biblical scholarship as Q, from the initial letter of *Quelle*, the German word for source). Incidentally, the very assumption that there must be a **written** collection of sayings, labeled Q, reflects the deep-seated literary bias in Bible scholarship. The lack of an actual written text of Q has not prevented scholars from writing learned discussions of the presumed form and contents of Q (cf. Kloppenborg 1994). Relatively few Bible experts have "questioned whether Q circulated in a written form, or whether it was not perhaps an oral collection of sayings" (Koch 1969:87). These efforts to probe the stylistic and ideological characteristics of J, E, P, D, and Q, among others, have preoccupied Bible scholars for decades, but this is not my concern here. I intend to consider the Bible as it exists as a final product. I leave matters of source criticism to those better qualified to investigate such issues. Now I wish to resume consideration of the endless number of multiple versions of elements in the Bible.

In Genesis, we find another fascinating set of texts that include a numerical facet. There are several diverse accounts of the trees in the Garden of Eden that differ with respect to whether man was permitted to eat their fruits. Here are those accounts:

> *And God said, Behold, I have given you every herb bearing seed, which is upon the face of all the earth, and **every tree**, in the which is the fruit of a tree yielding seed; to you it shall be for meat* (Gen. 1:29).

The implication here is that man is free to eat any tree bearing fruit, with no exceptions. In the second chapter of Genesis, however, we find a different version, with two specific trees named:

> *And out of the ground made the Lord God to grow every tree that is pleasant to the sight, and good for food; the tree of life also in the midst of the garden and the tree of knowledge of good and evil* (Gen. 2:9).

In a later account, there is only one tree that is off limits, whose fruit is forbidden:

> And the Lord God commanded the man, saying, Of every tree of the garden thou mayest freely eat: But of the tree of the knowledge of good and evil, thou shalt not eat of it: for in the day that thou eatest thereof thou shalt surely die (Gen. 2:16–17).

Adam, influenced by Eve, who was influenced by the serpent, eats the fruit of the forbidden tree, not named in the Bible, but traditionally said to be an apple. God punishes the couple by banishing them from the Garden of Eden, but he does so in part for fear that they will eat of another tree, namely, the tree of life:

> And the Lord God said, Behold, the man is become as one of us, to know good and evil: and now, lest he put forth his hand, and take also of the tree of life, and eat, and live for ever: Therefore the Lord God sent him forth from the garden of Eden to till the ground from whence he was taken (Gen. 3:22).

But in the earlier versions, either the fruit of **every** tree could be eaten by man, or the fruit of every tree **except for one,** the tree of the knowledge of good and evil, could be eaten by man. In this last version, there is apparently the fruit of another tree that God does not wish man to eat, namely, the one that would give humans immortality. It is the forfeiture of this tree that makes the Garden of Eden narrative an example of an origin of death myth. In terms of numerical variation, we have different numbers of trees forbidden to man: none, one, and two.

Another instance of number variation occurs when Jesus drives devils out of a distraught or disturbed human into a group of swine. According to Mark and Luke, the incident took place in *"the country of the Gadarenes"* (Mark 5:1; Luke 8:26). There Jesus met *"out of the tombs **a man** with an unclean spirit"* (Mark 5:2) or *"**a certain man,** which had devils long time, and ware no clothes, neither abode in any house, but in the tombs"* (Luke 8:27). Matthew's version differs: *"And when he was come to the other side into the country of the Gergesenes, there met him **two** possessed with devils, coming out of the tombs"* (Matt. 8:28). Was there one man possessed or two men possessed? (And did the incident take place in the country of the Gadarenes or the Gergesenes?)

Other miraculous cures reflect similar numerical variation. Matthew

(20:30) reports that Jesus restored the sight of **two** blind men, but Mark (10:46) and Luke (18:35) in their versions of the same incident indicate that only **one** blind man was involved.

> *And as they **departed from Jericho**, a great multitude followed him. And, beyond, two blind men sitting by the wayside. . . . So Jesus had compassion on them and touched their eyes: and immediately their eyes received sight* (Matt. 20:29, 30, 34).

> *And it came to pass, that as **he was come nigh into Jericho**, a certain blind **man** sat by the wayside begging. . . . And Jesus said unto him, Receive thy sight: thy faith hath saved thee* (Luke 18:35, 42).

In addition to the numerical disparity between curing two blind men versus one blind man, we also have variation with respect to whether the cure took place upon Jesus' departure from Jericho or after his arrival at Jericho. Mark's version offers something of a composite compromise:

> *And they **came to Jericho**: and as he went out of Jericho with his disciples and a great number of people, blind Bartimeus, the son of Timeus, sat by the highway side begging. . . . And Jesus said unto him, Go thy way; thy faith hath made thee whole. And immediately he received his sight* (Mark 10:46, 52).

An even more interesting instance of variation with respect to number may be found in the four different versions describing who came to the sepulchre where the body of Christ was entombed. One should keep in mind that the four Gospels, from a folkloristic perspective, are four versions of the same basic narrative and that, accordingly, we should expect to find such variation.

According to John (20:1),

> *The first day of the week cometh Mary Magdalene early, when it was yet dark unto the sepulchre.*

So we have **one** woman as a visitor. But according to Matthew (28:1),

> *In the end of the sabbath, as it began to dawn toward the first day of the week, came Mary Magdalene and the other Mary to see the sepulchre.*

So we have **two** women as visitors. However, according to Mark (16:1–2),

> And when the sabbath was past, Mary Magdalene, and Mary the mother of James, and Salome, had bought sweet spices, that they might come and anoint him, and very early in the morning, the first day of the week, they came unto the sepulchre at the rising of the sun.

So we have **three** women as visitors. Finally, according to Luke (24:1, 9–10):

> Now upon the first day of the week, very early in the morning, they came unto the sepulchre, bringing the spices which they had prepared and certain others with them. . . . And returned from the sepulchre and told all these things unto the eleven, and to all the rest. It was Mary Magdalene, and Joanna, and Mary the mother of James, and other women that were with them which told these things unto the apostles.

So we have **four** or more women as visitors. (It is also noteworthy that there is variation with respect to the time of the visit. According to John (20:1), it occurred "*when it was yet dark*," but according to Mark (16:2), the visit took place "*at the rising of the sun*.")

However many women came to the sepulchre, there is some dispute about what they observed there, specifically the number of men or angels and whether these men or angels were sitting or standing. According to Matthew (28:2–6),

> And, behold, there was a great earthquake: for the angel of the Lord descended from heaven, and came and rolled back the stone from the door, and **sat** upon it. His countenance was like lightning and his raiment white as snow.

So there is a single angel at the sepulchre and he is seated. Mark, in contrast, speaks of a young man rather than an angel. He too is seated.

> And entering into the sepulchre, they saw a young man **sitting** on the right side, clothed in a long white garment (16:5).

Luke also speaks of men rather than angels, but he mentions two men, not one:

*And they found the stone rolled away from the sepulchre. And they entered in, and found not the body of the Lord Jesus. And it came to pass, as they were much perplexed thereabout, behold **two men stood** by them in shining garments (24:2–4).*

Note that the two men are standing, not sitting. John agrees with Luke with respect to number, but in his report, it is angels, not men, and they are sitting, not standing.

*But Mary stood without at the sepulchre weeping: and as she wept, she stooped down, and looked into the sepulchre. And seeth **two angels in** white, **sitting**, the one at the head, and the other at the feet, where the body of Jesus had lain (20:11–12).*

If we summarize these four reports, we learn that whoever came to the sepulchre saw one or two men, or one or two angels, either sitting or standing. This may well present a problem for the historian looking for the "correct" number of men or angels in one posture or another, but it is perfectly normal for the folklorist, who would be surprised if there were not such variation encountered in four different versions of the same legend. Indeed, from a purely folkloristic perspective, it is utter folly to attempt to reconcile such diversity. Each of the four versions has its own integrity. One should keep in mind that in folklore there is no one correct version; there are only alternative versions. This is precisely why oral history is so often the despair of historians, who are distinctly uncomfortable when confronted with different oral historical accounts of the same event. In contrast, the folklorist may be disappointed if there is insufficient variation. The very variation that bedevils historians is considered an asset to the folklorist, an asset that attests to the folkloricity of the item in question.

Another interesting instance of numerical variation occurs in the dramatic prediction made by Jesus that Peter would deny him three times before the cock crowed, that is, presumably before the next morning.

Jesus said unto him, Verily I say unto thee, That this night, before the cock crow, thou shalt deny me thrice. . . . And after a while came unto him they that stood by, and said to Peter, Surely thou also art one of them; for thy speech betrayeth thee. Then began he to curse and to swear, saying, I know not the man, and immediately the cock crew. And Peter remembered the word of Jesus, which said unto him, Before the cock crow, thou shalt deny me thrice. And he went out, and wept bitterly (Matt. 26:34, 73–75).

John's account is similar, except the last accuser is said to be a relative of the man whose ear Peter had cut off:

> *Jesus answered him, Wilt thou lay down thy life for my sake? Verily, verily, I say unto thee, The cock shall not crow, till thou hast denied me thrice. . . . One of the servants of the high priest, **being his kinsman whose ear Peter had cut off,** saith, Did not I see thee in the garden with him? Peter then denied again; and immediately the cock crew* (John 13:38, 18:26–27).

Luke's version is also similar, except it reports that Jesus actually was present at Peter's third denial and that he looked at Peter. The other versions present Peter alone as he realized his repeated failure to acknowledge his association with Jesus.

> *And he said, I tell thee, Peter, the cock shall not crow this day, before that thou shalt thrice deny that thou knowest me . . . and about the space of one hour after another confidently affirmed, saying, Of a truth this fellow also was with him; for he is a Galilean. And Peter said, Man, I know not what thou sayest. And immediately, while he yet spake, the cock crew. **And the Lord turned, and looked upon Peter.** And Peter remembered the word of the Lord, how he had said unto him, Before the cock crow, thou shalt deny me thrice. And Peter went out, and wept bitterly* (Luke 22:34, 59–62).

The numerical variation is found in Mark's version, in which the cock crows not once but twice:

> *And Jesus saith unto him, Verily I say unto thee, That this day, even in this night, before the cock crow **twice,** thou shalt deny me thrice. . . . And as Peter was beneath in the palace, there cometh one of the maids of the high priest: And when she saw Peter warming himself, she looked upon him, and said, And thou also wast with Jesus of Nazareth. But he denied, saying, I know not, neither understand I what thou sayest. And he went out into the porch; and the cock crew . . . And a little after, they that stood by said again to Peter, Surely thou art one of them: for thou art a Galilean, and thy speech agreeth thereto. But he began to curse and to swear, saying, I know not this man of whom ye speak. **And the second time the cock crew.** And Peter called to mind the word that Jesus said unto him, Before the cock crow twice, thou shalt deny me thrice. And when he thought thereon, he wept* (Mark 14:30, 66–68, 70–72).

Did the cock crow once or twice? Was Peter by himself when he realized that Christ had accurately predicted that his desire for self-preservation would be stronger than his avowed loyalty to Jesus, or was Jesus present at Peter's last denial, giving him a knowing look?

There are simply too many examples of numerical discrepancies to enumerate. A few more illustrations should suffice. One such discrepancy, perhaps a minor and somewhat trivial one, concerns the age at which the sons of Levi are supposed to begin their special service. According to Numbers 4:3, "*From **thirty years old** and upward even until fifty years old, all that enter into the host to do the work in the tabernacle of the congregation.*" This number or age is confirmed by 1 Chronicles 23:3: "*Now the Levites were numbered from the age of **thirty years** and upward.*" But Numbers 8:23–24 differs: "*And the Lord spake unto Moses saying, This is it that belongeth unto the Levites: from **twenty and five years old** and upward they shall go in to wait upon the service of the tabernacle of the congregation.*" In Ezra 3:8, we are told that the Levites were appointed "*from **twenty years old** and upward, to set forward the work of the house of the Lord.*" So do Levites begin their service at age twenty, twenty-five, or thirty? Small point, but once again an illustration of how oral accounts were never reconciled, thereby allowing the discrepancy to remain set forever in print.

Sometimes the numerical discrepancy refers to the age of an individual. For example, consider the following two versions describing the age of Ahaziah when he assumed the throne:

> **Two and twenty years old** *was Ahaziah when he began to reign; and he reigned one year in Jerusalem. And his mother's name was Athaliah, the daughter of Omri king of Israel* (2 Kings 8:26).

> **Forty and two years old** *was Ahaziah when he began to reign, and he reigned one year in Jerusalem. His mother's name also was Athaliah the daughter of Omri* (2 Chron. 22:2).

No doubt there are those who would see this as nothing more than scribal error, but the fact that such "errors" occur throughout the Bible and the fact that such discrepancies are a commonplace in folklore suggest that the variation is not to be explained away as simply scribal error.

Sometimes the numerical variation concerns the number of prisoners or captives taken in a war or after a siege. For example, when Nebuchadnezzar, the king of Babylon, successfully laid siege to the city of Jerusalem, he took a large number of Jews back to Babylon. The question is, How many Jews did he take?

*This is the people whom Nebuchadrezzar carried away captive: in the seventh year **three thousand Jews and three and twenty** (Jer. 52:28).*

*At that time the servants of Nebuchadnezzar king of Babylon came up against Jerusalem, and the city was besieged. . . . And he carried away all Jerusalem, and all the princes, and all the mighty men of valor **even ten thousand captives**, and all the craftsmen and smiths: none remained, save the poorest sort of the people of the land* (2 Kings 24:11, 14).

*And all the men of might **even seven thousand**, and craftsmen and smiths **a thousand**, all that were strong and apt for war, even them the king of Babylon brought captive to Babylon* (2 Kings 24:16).

Wartime statistics are notoriously unreliable and inevitably subject to propagandistic inflation, but still, there is a considerable difference between slightly more than three thousand captives on the one hand, and either eight (seven plus one) thousand or ten thousand on the other. Here is another example of a statistical discrepancy. In the time of King David, one report indicated that some **eighteen thousand** Edomites were slain in the valley of salt (1 Chronicles 18:12), whereas the preamble to Psalm 60 reported that **twelve thousand** Edomites in the valley of salt were killed.

There are dozens of duplicate texts or passages in the Bible. The sacredness of the Bible may have prevented would-be editors from deleting such obvious duplicates. It would have been a sacrilege to delete them, and there would have been the additional practical problem of deciding which of the duplicates to delete. It is perhaps worth noting that the last lines of the last book of the Bible specifically warn against either adding anything to or eliminating any words from the text: "*For I testify unto every man that heareth the words of the prophecy of this book, If any man shall add unto these things, God shall add unto him the plagues that are written in this book: And if any man shall take away from the words of the book of this prophecy, God shall take away his part out of the book of life . . .*" (Rev. 22:18–19). A comparable admonition appears in the Old Testament: "*Ye shall not add unto the word which I command you, neither shall ye diminish aught from it, that ye make keep the commands of the Lord your God which I command you*" (Deut. 4:2).

Similarly, "*What thing soever I command you, observe to do it: thou shalt not add thereto, nor diminish from it*" (Deut. 12:32).

One of the most detailed texts consists of the second chapter of Ezra (2:1–70) and most of the seventh chapter of Nehemiah (7:6–73). More than thirty families are enumerated together with their numbers. It would be terribly tedious to compare the entire lists of all the families mentioned, but it might be useful to study a random sample of nine of them. The numerical discrepancies are highlighted.

Ezra 2:7–16	*Nehemiah 7:12–21*
The children of Elam, a thousand two hundred fifty and four.	The children of Elam, a thousand two hundred fifty and four.
The children of Zattu, **nine** hundred forty and five.	The children of Zattu, **eight** hundred forty and five.
The children of Zaccai, seven hundred and threescore.	The children of Zaccai, seven hundred and threescore.
The children of **Bani,** six hundred forty and **two.**	The children of **Binnu,** six hundred forty and **eight.**
The children of Bebai, six hundred twenty and **three.**	The children of Bebai, six hundred twenty and **eight.**
The children of Azgad, **a** thousand **two** hundred twenty and two.	The children of Azgad, **two** thousand **three** hundred twenty and two.
The children of Adonikam, six hundred sixty and **six.**	The children of Adonikam, six hundred threescore and **seven.**
The children of Bigvai, two thousand **fifty and six.**	The children of Bigvai, two thousand **threescore and seven.**
The children of Adin, **four** hundred fifty and **four.**	The children of Adin, **six** hundred fifty and **five.**

The two lists are clearly two versions of the same basic census. It may be instructive to compare the final sections of these two chapters wherein the various contributions to the temple treasury are summarized:

> *And some of the chief of the fathers, when they came to the house of the Lord which is at Jerusalem, offered freely for the house of God to set it up in his place: They gave after their ability unto the treasure of the work* **threescore and one thousand drams** *of gold, and* **five thousand pounds** *of silver, and* **one hundred** *priests' garments* (Ezra 2:68–69).

> *And some of the chief of the fathers gave unto the work. The Tirshatha gave to the treasure* **a thousand drams** *of gold, fifty basins,* **five hundred and thirty** *priests' garments. And some of the chief of the fathers gave to the treasure of the work* **twenty thousand drams** *of gold, and* **two thousand and two hundred pounds** *of silver. And that which the rest of the people gave was* **twenty thousand drams** *of gold, and* **two thousand pounds** *of silver, and* **threescore and seven** *priests' garments* (Neh. 7:70–72).

These two passages provide a dramatic example of multiple existence and variation. Indeed, the second passage itself would seem to contain at least two if not three versions of the contributions to the treasure. The threefold formulaic pattern established in the Ezra version consists of (1) gold, (2) silver, and (3) priests' garments. The same structural formula appears three times (with some omissions) in the Nehemiah passage. But even without the assumption of multiple versions contained in the latter, the existence of both the Ezra and Nehemiah versions, coming as they do at the end of duplicate chapters, attests to the traditionality of the accounts.

Another set of multiple versions with numerical variation consists of the accounts of the multiplication of bread and fishes. We may begin with one of the versions reported by Matthew:

> *And when it was evening, his disciples came to him, saying, This is a desert place, and the time is now past; send the multitude away, that they may go into the villages, and buy themselves victuals. But Jesus said unto them, They need not depart; give ye them to eat. And they say unto him, We have here but* **five** *loaves, and* **two** *fishes. He said, Bring them hither to me. And he commanded the multitude to sit down on the grass, and took the* **five** *loaves and the* **two** *fishes, and looking up to heaven, he blessed, and brake, and gave the loaves to his disciples, and the disciples to the multitude. And they did all eat, and were filled: and they took up of the fragments that remained* **twelve** *baskets full. And they that had eaten were about* **five thousand** *men, beside women and children. And straightaway Jesus constrained his disciples to get into a ship and to go before him unto the other side, while he sent the multitudes away* (Matt. 14:15–22).

In the very next chapter of Matthew, we find a second version:

> Then Jesus called his disciples unto him, and said, I have compassion on
> the multitude, because they continue with me now three days, and have
> nothing to eat: and I will not send them away fasting, lest they faint in the
> way. And his disciples say unto him, Whence should we have so much bread
> in the wilderness, as to fill so great a multitude? And Jesus saith unto them,
> How many loaves have ye? and they said, **seven**, and **a few** little fishes. And
> he commanded the multitude to sit down on the ground. And he took the
> **seven** loaves and the fishes, and gave thanks, and brake them, and gave his
> disciples, and the disciples to the multitude. And they did all eat, and were
> filled: and they took up of the broken meat that was left **seven** baskets full,
> and they that did eat were **four** thousand men, beside women and children
> and he sent away the multitude, and took ship, and came into the coasts of
> Magdala (Matt. 15:32–39).

The differences in these two versions are primarily concerned with
numbers: five versus seven loaves of bread; two versus a few fish, twelve
versus seven baskets of leftovers, and five thousand versus four thousand men fed. The argument that these two accounts represent totally
different events would not be persuasive to anyone with the slightest
familiarity with folklore. Not only is the basic structure of the legend
similar, but even the wording of the specific details—for example, so
many men *"beside women and children"*—and the concluding element
of sending the multitudes away and taking ship confirm the cognation
of the two texts. From a folkloristic perspective, it is perfectly obvious
that we have two versions of one and the same event (cf. Bultmann
1963:217; Anderson 1985:80–82; Helms 1988:75).

In Luke's account, we have just one version in which there are five
loaves, two fishes, five thousand men, and twelve baskets of leftovers
(Luke 9:10–17). In John's report, there are again five loaves, but we are
told they are barley loaves for five thousand men with twelve baskets
of leftovers (John 6:5–13). From this, we might well assume that the
second version in Matthew is an anomaly, a departure from the normal
form of the legend. Fortunately, Mark, like Matthew, presents two different versions:

> And when the day was now spent, his disciples came unto him, and said,
> This is a desert place, and now the time is far passed: Send them away, that
> they may go into the country road about, and into the villages, and buy
> themselves bread: for they have nothing to eat. He answered and said unto

them, Give ye them to eat. And they say unto him, Shall we go and buy two hundred pennyworth of bread, and give them to eat. He saith unto them, How many loaves have ye? go and see. And when they knew, they say, **Five** *and* **two** *fishes. And he commanded them to make all sit down by companies upon the green grass. And they sat down in ranks, by hundreds, and by fifties. And when he had taken the* **five** *loaves, and the* **two** *fishes, he looked up to heaven, and blessed, and brake the loaves, and gave them to his disciples to set before them; and the* **two** *fishes divided he among them all. And they did all eat, and were filled. And they took up* **twelve** *baskets full of the fragments, and of the fishes. And they that did eat of the loaves were about* **five** *thousand men. And straightway he constrained his disciples to get into the ship, and to go to the other side before unto Bethsaida while he sent away the people* (Mark 6:35–45).

This first version in Mark closely resembles the first version in Matthew, but it is not identical. In Mark's version, the multitude is seated in ranks by hundreds and by fifties, a detail not found in Matthew's version. Here is Mark's second version:

In those days the multitude being very great, and having nothing to eat, Jesus called his disciples unto him and saith unto them, I have compassion on the multitude because they have been with me three days, and have nothing to eat. And if I send them away fasting to their own houses, they will faint by the way: for divers of them came from far. And his disciples answered him, From whence can a man satisfy these men with bread here in the wilderness? And he asked them, How many loaves have ye? And they said, **Seven.** *And he commanded the people to sit down on the ground: and he took the* **seven** *loaves, and gave thanks, and brake, and gave to his disciples to set before them; and they did set them before the people. And they had a few small fishes; and he blessed, and commanded to set them also before them. So they did eat, and were filled: and they took up of the broken meat that was left* **seven** *baskets. And they that had eaten were about* **four** *thousand: and he sent them away. And straightway he entered a ship with his disciples, and came into the parts of Dalmanutha* (Mark 8:1–10).

This second version of Mark is very similar to the second version of Matthew, with only minor differences, such as serving the bread first and the fishes second rather than both at once, and departing by ship for Dalmanutha instead of Magdala. What is perhaps most interesting of all is the fact that both Matthew and Mark were apparently aware of the differences between the two accounts:

Do ye not yet understand, neither remember the five loaves of the five thousand, and how many baskets ye took up? Neither the seven loaves of the four thousand, and how many baskets ye took up? (Matt. 16:9–10).

Having eyes, see ye not? and having ears, hear ye not? and do ye not remember? When I brake the five loaves among five thousand, how many baskets full of fragments took ye up? They say unto him, Twelve. And when the seven among four thousand, how many baskets full of fragments took ye up? and they said, Seven (Mark 8:18–20).

Mark's version suggests Jesus is giving a quiz to his disciples to test their memories. But this effort to imply that there were two separate food-multiplying incidents cannot conceal the textual evidence pointing to the likelihood that both reports are referring to one and the same incident. If this were the only occurrence in the Bible of two or more versions of an incident, we might well question whether there were one or two events being described. But in the context of countless duplicate texts and multiple versions in the Bible, the logical inference is that this is another example of this common phenomenon.

The editorial rhetorical device of specifically drawing attention to parallel events does not succeed in disguising the fact that there are two or more different versions of the same story. We find this in the Old Testament accounts of crossing the Red Sea and the River Jordan:

And Moses stretched out his hand over the sea: and the Lord caused the sea to go back by a strong east wind all that night, and made the sea dry land, and the waters were divided. And the children of Israel went into the midst of the sea upon the dry ground: and the waters were a wall unto them on their right hand, and on their left (Exod. 14:21–22).

And it shall come to pass, as soon as the soles of the feet of the priests that bear the ark of the Lord, the Lord of all the earth, shall rest in the waters of Jordan, that the waters of Jordan shall be cut off from the waters that come down from above; and they shall stand upon a heap. . . . That the waters which came down from above stood and rose up upon a heap . . . and those that came down towards the sea of the plain, even the salt sea, failed, and were cut off and the people passed over right against Jericho. And the priests that bare the ark of the covenant of the Lord stood firm on dry ground in the midst of Jordan, and all the Israelites passed over on dry ground, until all the people were passed clean over Jordan (Josh. 3:13, 16–17).

When Joshua recounts this adventure to the children of Israel, he makes a direct comparison to the Red Sea miracle:

> *Then ye shall let your children know, saying, Israel came over this Jordan on dry land. For the Lord your God dried up the waters of Jordan from before you, until ye were passed over, as the Lord your God did to the Red sea, which he dried up from before us, until we were gone over* (Josh. 4:22–23).

Just as there were two versions of the multiplication of fishes and loaves narrative, so there are two versions of a miraculous crossing of a body of water.

Variation in Name

Names as well as numbers reveal variation and multiple existence. Sometimes it is just a matter of an alternate spelling of a particular name, but often it is a matter of two entirely distinct names, that is, two different individuals who are said to have performed a certain action. In the elevator-incident legend mentioned earlier, the African American man who pays the hotel bill of the racist women varies from version to version. Several multiple texts demonstrate this kind of variation.

Perhaps one of the most striking instances of different versions of the same story involving different names occurs in Genesis. There are three distinct versions of a narrative in which a man pretends that his wife is his sister. He does this for fear that the ruler of the land might kill him in order to take the man's wife for himself. Two of the versions involve Abraham and Sarah; the third involves Isaac and Rebekah. A comparison of the three versions with attention to the wording makes it obvious to any trained folklorist that the three versions are unquestionably cognate.

The first version of the narrative is set in Egypt with the Pharaoh as the misled male suitor of Sarah; the second version takes place in Gerar with Abimelech, the king of Gerar, as the victimized would-be husband of Sarah. The third version also is placed in Gerar with Abimelech again the duped prospective predator. In all cases, the sister masquerade is revealed and the initial marital bond remains intact.

Here are three versions of the story:

And it came to pass, when he was come near to enter into Egypt, that he said unto Sarai his wife, Behold now, I know that thou art a fair woman to look upon: therefore it shall come to pass when the Egyptians shall see thee, that they shall say, This is his wife: and they will kill me, but they will save thee alive. Say, I pray thee, thou art my sister: that it may be well with me for thy sake; and my soul shall live because of thee . . . and the woman was taken into Pharaoh's house. And he entreated Abram well for her sake: and he had sheep, and oxen, and he asses, and menservants, and maidservants, and she asses, and camels. And the Lord plagued Pharaoh and his house with great plagues, because of Sarai, Abram's wife. And Pharaoh called Abram and said, **What is this that thou has done unto me?** *Why didst thou not tell me that she was thy wife. Why saidst thou, She is my sister? so I might have taken her to me to wife: now therefore behold thy wife, take her and go thy way* (Gen. 12:11–13, 15–19).

The order of events varies slightly in the second version:

And Abraham said of Sarah his wife, She is my sister: and Abimelech king of Gerar sent, and took Sarah. But God came to Abimelech in a dream by night, and said to him, Behold, thou art but a dead man, for the woman which thou hast taken; for she is a man's wife. . . . Then Abimelech called Abraham and said unto him, **What hast thou done unto us?** *. . . And Abraham said, Because I thought, Surely the fear of God is not in this place; and they will slay me for my wife's sake. . . . And Abimelech took sheep, and oxen, and menservants, and women-servants, and gave them unto Abraham, and restored him Sarah his wife* (Gen. 20:2–3, 9, 11, 14).

The third version substitutes Isaac and Rebekah in place of Abraham and Sarah (Abram and Sarai), but the locale of Gerar remains the same, and Abimelech continues in the role of duped ruler. In this case, however, it is not God's message in a dream that reveals the duplicity, but Abimelech's direct observation of Isaac and Rebekah, whose overt behavior is evidently not that normally expected of brother and sister:

And Isaac dwelt in Gerar. And the men of the place asked him of his wife; and he said, She is my sister: for he feared to say, She is my wife; lest, said he, the men of the place should kill me for Rebekah; because she was fair to look upon. And it came to pass, when he had been there a long time, that Abimelech king of the Philistines looked out at a window, and saw, and, behold Isaac was sporting with Rebekah his wife. And Abimelech called Isaac, and said, Behold, of a surety she is thy wife: and how saidst thou, She is my sister? And Isaac said unto him, Because I said, Lest I die for her. And

*Abimelech said, **What is this thou hast done unto us?** one of the people might lightly have lain with thy wife, and thou shouldest have brought guiltiness upon us. And Abimelech charged all his people, saying, He that toucheth this man or his wife shall surely be put to death* (Gen. 26:6–11).

Not only are these three versions of the same story nearly identical with respect to basic plot, but the occurrence of set phrases also attests to their cognation:

What is this that thou has done unto me? (Gen. 12:18)

What has thou done unto us? (Gen. 20:9)

What is this thou hast done unto us? (Gen. 26:10)

Coincidence? I don't think so. And this is just one of many, many multiple versions of a narrative or episode in the Bible. Anyone the least bit familiar with folklore scholarship could not doubt for an instant that we have here three versions of the same story. Yet what is so patently obvious to the folklorist evidently is not to the Bible scholar. One such scholar who devoted an entire essay to the three versions made the following unequivocal statement: "Simply stated, the wife-sister texts do not now constitute the product or immediate residue of the oral story-telling institution" (Petersen 1973:32). Another critic takes the usual literary approach speaking of a single "author" constructing the three texts: "It . . . seems probable that the Biblical author must have had a standard 'type-scene' in mind when constructing each of them" (Gordis 1985:358). I would submit that this is not a "type-scene" involving completely different stories with roughly analogous plots. Rather, they are three versions of one and the same story. (For a discussion of the relative merits of both the oral and the literary approaches to this story, see Culley 1976b:40–41.)

Anyone who doubts that the identical incident involving a sister-wife deception is told of both Abraham and his son Isaac should also consider the fact that Abraham and Isaac apparently were each separately given credit for naming Beersheba after settling a dispute with Abimelech.

And it came to pass at that time that Abimelech and Phichol the chief captain of his host spake unto Abraham, saying, God is with thee in all that thou doest: Now therefore swear unto me here by God, that thou wilt not deal falsely with me. . . . And Abraham said, I will swear. . . . And Abraham took sheep and oxen and gave them unto Abimelech; and both of them made a covenant. And Abraham set seven ewe lambs of the flock by themselves. . . . And he said, For these seven ewe lambs shalt thou take of my hand, that they may be a witness unto me, that I have digged this well. Wherefore he called that place Beersheba; because there they sware both of them (Gen. 21:22, 23, 24, 27, 30–31).

Isaac had a strikingly similar encounter with Abimelech:

Then Abimelech went to him from Gerar, and Ahuzzath one of his friends, and Phichol the chief captain of his army. And Isaac said unto them, Wherefore come ye to me, seeing ye hate me, and have sent me away from you. And they said, We saw certainly that the Lord was with thee: and we said, Let there be now an oath betwixt us, even betwixt us and thee, and let us make a covenant with thee; That thou will do us no hurt. . . . And it came to pass the same day that Isaac's servants came, and told him concerning the well which they had digged, and said unto him, We have found water. And he called it Shebah: therefore the name of the city is Beersheba unto this day (Gen. 26:26–27, 28, 32–33).

The double naming of Beersheba is also apparent inasmuch as Isaac is reported to have proceeded "to Beersheba" (Gen. 26:23) **before** he is credited with giving it that name (Gen. 26:33). There can be no doubt that we have two distinct versions of the same place-naming incident involving Abimelech and Phichol, the chief captain of his army.

There are duplicate texts in the memorable story of the parting of the Red Sea. Compare two passages in Exodus 14:

And the children of Israel went into the midst of the sea upon the dry ground: and the waters were a wall unto them on their right hand, and on their left (Exod. 14:22).

But the children of Israel walked upon dry land in the midst of the sea; and the waters were a wall unto them on their right hand, and on their left (Exod. 14:29).

The passages are very similar except for a minor difference in sequence. In the first passage, "*midst of the sea*" comes before "*dry ground,*" whereas in the second passages "*dry land*" comes before "*midst of the sea.*" I shall have more to say about variations in sequence later in this essay. What I wish to discuss now is the comparison of the song of praise that follows this miraculous event. Both accounts occur in Exodus 15:

> *Then sang **Moses** and children of Israel this song unto the Lord, and spake, saying, I will sing unto the Lord, for he hath triumphed gloriously: the horse and his rider hath he thrown into the sea* (Exod. 15:1).

> *And **Miriam** the Prophetess, the sister of Aaron, took a timbrel in her hand: and all the women went out after her with timbrels and with dances.: And Miriam answered them, Sing ye to the Lord, for he hath triumphed gloriously: the horse and his rider hath he thrown into the sea* (Exod. 15:20–21).

In the first version, it is Moses who led the celebratory singing; in the second version, it is Miriam, the sister of Aaron. Incidentally, this variation would tend to support Friedman's hypothesis in *Who Wrote the Bible?*, namely, that the different strands or voices in the Old Testament were divided in part with respect to those who favored Moses and those who were partisan to Aaron and Miriam (1989:76–79, 190, 196–98).

Sometimes it is not the name of an individual that varies, but the name of a whole group. For example, when Joseph's brothers take from him his famous coat of many colors and throw him into an empty pit, they then proceed to sell him to an itinerant group bound for Egypt. The question is, What was the name of that itinerant group? According to one version, the brothers "*lifted up their eyes and looked, and behold, a company of Ishmaelites came from Gilead, with their camels bearing spicery and balm and myrrh, going to carry it down to Egypt. . . . Come, and let us sell him to the Ishmaelites . . . and they drew and lifted up Joseph out of the pit, and sold Joseph to the Ishmaelites for twenty pieces of silver: and they brought Joseph into Egypt*" (Gen. 37:25, 27, 28). This passage indicates that it was the **Ishmaelites** who brought Joseph to Egypt. But the same chapter of Genesis contains a second version of the event. "*Then there passed by Midianites merchantmen. . . . And the Midianites sold him [Joseph] into Egypt unto Potiphar, an officer of Pharaoh's, and captain of the guard*" (Gen. 37:28, 36). The second version indicates that it was the **Midianites** who brought Joseph to Egypt.

Another striking illustration of a discrepancy with respect to a name or a personage involved in an incident is to be found in the events recounted in 2 Samuel 24, events that appear in a second version as 1

Chronicles 21:1–27. Both versions begin with King David receiving a request to carry out a census of Israel, but the request comes from two very different sources:

> *And again the anger of the **Lord** was kindled against Israel, and he moved David against them to say, Go number Israel and Judah* (2 Sam. 24:1).

> *And **Satan** stood up against Israel, and provoked David to number Israel* (1 Chron. 21:1).

It would be a mistake to claim that the difference of just one name in this case constitutes only a trivial variation. There is surely a world of difference between God and the devil! In any case, whoever it was who ordered David to take a census, there are divergent reports of the results of that census. In both versions, David asks his captain Joab to make a head count.

> *And Joab gave up the sum of the number of the people unto the king: and there were in Israel **eight hundred thousand** valiant men that drew the sword; and the men of Judah were **five hundred thousand** men* (2 Sam. 24:9).

> *And Joab gave the sum of the number of the people unto David. And they of Israel were **a thousand thousand and a hundred thousand** men that drew sword: and Judah was **four hundred threescore and ten thousand** men that drew sword* (1 Chron. 21:5).

Sometimes the variation is limited to the name of a single individual. For example, in the very beginning of Matthew, the genealogy of Jesus is traced—in this case, through Mary, the mother of Jesus—all the way back to Abraham. Included in Matthew is: *"And **Ozias** begat **Joatham"** (Matt. 1:9). These names differ slightly from those reported by Isaiah, who spoke of *"**Jotham**, the son of **Uzziah**, king of Judah"* (7:1; cf. Isa. 1:1, 6:1). These names are confirmed elsewhere: *"So **Uzziah** slept with his fathers. . . . He is a leper: and **Jotham** his son reigned in his stead"* (2 Chron. 26:23) and also *"began **Jotham** the son of **Uzziah** king of Judah to reign"* (2 Kings 15:32).

On the other hand, in the very same chapter, we are told that it was **Azariah** who was a leper and who was succeeded by his son **Jotham.** *"And the Lord smote the king, so that he was a leper unto the day of his* *death, and dwelt in a several house. And **Jotham** the king's son was over the house, judging the people of the land. So **Azariah** slept with his fathers . . . and **Jotham** his son reigned in his stead"* (2 Kings 15:5, 7). The name Azariah occurs elsewhere, as, for example, in another listing of David and Solomon's progeny, we find *"**Azariah** his son, **Jotham** his son"* (1 Chron. 23:12).

What is the upshot of all this? Pretty clearly, Ozias, Uzziah, and Azariah are the names of one and the same person. How can we account for the variation? Once again, we as folklorists can explain such variation as resulting from the typical oral transmission process. The fact that chapter 15 of 2 Kings **begins** with a reference to **Azariah** (2 Kings 15:1) and **ends** with a reference to **Uzziah** (2 Kings 15:32) strongly suggests that at least two different oral sources were combined in composing this chapter.

There are other instances of variations in the spelling of names in the Bible. In 1 Chronicles, for example, we have three different accounts of the descendants of Caleb. This includes three diverse renderings of the name of one of his wives or concubines:

> *And when Azubah was dead, and Caleb took unto him **Ephrath**, which bare him Hur* (1 Chron. 2:19).

> *And **Ephah**, Caleb's concubine, bare Haran* (1 Chron. 2:46).

> *These were the sons of Caleb the son of Hur, the firstborn of **Ephratah*** (1 Chron. 2:50).

In this instance, we simply have three different versions of the name of someone who appears to be the same woman. There are countless such minor variations of names in the Bible. A curious example is found in the two versions of the visit of the Queen of Sheba to King Solomon. In one version, we find the following passage:

> *And the servants also of **Huram**, and the servants of Solomon, which brought gold from Ophir, brought **algum** trees and precious stones* (2 Chron. 9:10).

But the analogous passage in the second version differs slightly:

> *And the navy also of **Hiram**, that brought gold from Ophir, brought in from Ophir great plenty of **almug** trees and precious stones* (1 Kings 10:11).

The alternation of "Huram" and "Hiram" is trivial, but the transposition of "g" and "m" is more striking. The proper term for the tree in question is apparently "algum," but the weight of biblical authority is so great that the probable misrendering of "algum" into "almug" has been retained; "almug" is even listed as a word in the *Oxford English Dictionary*.

Some examples of name variation are even more extreme. One obvious illustration concerns the name of King David's second son. While David was living in Hebron, he had six sons by six different wives. In two versions of a description of his Hebron family, there is agreement about five of these sons, but a disparity with regard to one of them.

> *And unto David were sons born in Hebron . . . and his second,* **Chileab,** *of Abigail, the wife of Nabal the Carmelite* (2 Sam. 3:2, 3).

> *Now these were the sons of David, which were born unto him in Hebron . . . the second* **Daniel,** *of Abigail the Carmelitess* (1 Chron. 3:1).

So was the name of David's second son born in Hebron "Chileab" or "Daniel"? Two versions, two names.

There are many such variations in names. For example, what was the name of Abijah or Abijam's maternal grandfather?

> *Now in the eighteenth year of king Jeroboam began Abijah to reign over Judah. He reigned three years in Jerusalem. His mother's name also was Michajah the daughter of* **Uriel** *of Gibeah* (2 Chron. 13:1–2).

> *Now in the eighteenth year of king Jeroboam, the son of Nebat reigned Abijam over Judah. Three years reigned he in Jerusalem. And his mother's name was Maachah, the daughter of* **Abishalom** (1 Kings 15:1–2).

We have a third version in which Rehoboam took as one of his wives *"Maachah the daughter of* **Absalom;** *which bare him Abijah"* (2 Chron. 11:18). So was the name of Abijah/Abijam's maternal grandfather "Uriel" or "Abishalom/Absalom"? Different versions, different names.

In the same vein, what was the name of Jair's father?

> *And Moses gave Gilead unto Machir the son of Manasseh; and he dwelt therein. And Jair the son of* **Manasseh** *went and took the small towns thereof* (Num. 32:40–1).

> *And afterward Hezron went in to the daughter of Machir the father of Gilead, whom he married when he was threescore years old; and she bare him Segub. And Segub begat Jair, who had three and twenty cities in the land of Gilead* (1 Chron. 2:21–2).

So was Jair's father's name "Manasseh" or "Segub"? Two versions, two names.

No doubt one of the classic cases of name variation in the Bible concerns the name of Moses' father-in-law. There are three possibilities. In the second chapter of Exodus, we learn that Moses fled from Egypt after slaying an Egyptian who was beating up a Jew. He sought refuge *"in the land of Midian,"* where he sat down by a well. There the seven daughters of the priest of Midian came to draw water, but they were driven off by a group of shepherds. Moses came to their rescue and helped them water their father's flock. And when the girls *"came to Reuel their father,"* he asked them why they had returned early.

> *And they said, An Egyptian delivered us out of the hand of the shepherds, and also drew water enough for us, and watered the flock. And he said unto his daughters, And where is he? why is it that ye have left the man? call him, that he may eat bread. And Moses was content to dwell with the man: and he gave Moses Zipporah his daughter* (Exod. 2:19–21).

This seems straightforward enough. Moses marries **Zipporah,** the daughter of **Reuel.** However, the very next chapter of Exodus begins as follows:

> *Now Moses kept the flock of **Jethro** his father-in-law, the priest of Midian* (Exod. 3:1).

So now it appears that the name of Moses' father-in-law is Jethro, not Reuel. Of course, in Old Testament times, polygamy was practiced, so perhaps it is simply a matter of Moses' having two wives. In that case, it would be perfectly understandable if he had two fathers-in-law. It is somewhat striking, however, that both Reuel and Jethro are described as being priests of Midian. It is even more remarkable once we learn the name of Jethro's daughter:

> *And Moses went and returned to Jethro his father-in-law, and said unto him, Let me go, I pray thee, and return unto my brethren which are in Egypt, and see whether they be yet alive. And Jethro said to Moses, Go in*

*peace. . . . And Moses took his wife and his sons, and set them upon an ass, and he returned to the land of Egypt. . . . Then **Zipporah** took a sharp stone and cut off the foreskin of her son, and cast it at this feet, and said, Surely a bloody husband art thou to me* (Exod. 4:18, 20, 25).

What are the mathematical chances of Moses marrying two different women, both daughters of priests of Midian, and both named Zipporah? Moses later sends Zipporah back to Jethro, presumably for safety's sake.

Then Jethro, Moses' father-in-law, took Zipporah, Moses' wife, after he had sent her back (Exod. 18:2).

Since the name Jethro occurs in three different chapters of Exodus, we might tend to favor that name over Reuel. However, the whole issue of the name of Moses' father-in-law is clouded further by a passage in Judges:

*Now Heber the Kenite, which was of the children of **Hobab the father-in-law of Moses**, had severed himself from the Kenites. . . .* (Judg. 4:11).

This name recurs in Numbers:

*And Moses said unto **Hobab**, the son of Raguel the Midianite, **Moses' father-in-law**. . . .* (Numb. 10:29).

So we have all told three different versions of the name of Moses' father-in-law: Reuel, Jethro, and Hobab.

Perhaps it is not so important to ascertain the name of Moses' father-in-law, but what about the name of Jesus' paternal grandfather? In Matthew's genealogy, the name is Jacob:

*And **Jacob** begat Joseph the husband of Mary, of whom was born Jesus, who is called Christ* (Matt. 1:16).

Luke's genealogy indicates a different name:

*And Jesus himself began to be about thirty years of age, being (as was supposed) the son of Joseph, which was the son of **Heli*** (Luke 3:23).

So was the name of Jesus' paternal grandfather "Jacob" or "Heli"? Two different versions of the genealogy, two different names!

On the subject of names, we might briefly consider the names of the twelve tribes of Israel and the names of the twelve disciples. A not so obvious but nevertheless clear-cut pair of duplicate texts in the Old Testament consists of Jacob's last words and Moses' last words (Genesis 49:1–28; Deuteronomy 33:1–26). Both texts delineate a list of heirs accompanied by predictions of their fates.

Jacob's List	*Moses' List*
Reuben	Reuben
Simeon and Levi	Judah and Levi
Judah	Benjamin
Zebulun	Joseph
Isachar	Zebulun
Dan	Isachar
Gad	Gad
Asher	Dan
Naphtali	Naphtali
Joseph	Asher
Benjamin	Jeshurun

We are told that *"All these are the twelve tribes of Israel"* (Gen. 49:28). But the lists are not identical. Simeon appears on Jacob's list, yet not on Moses' list. Jeshurun appears on Moses' list, but not on Jacob's list. Still, eleven of the twelve names are the same, and some of them are listed in the same sequence. Presumably this could be attributed to the fact that there are only twelve tribes. However, although the blessings for each individual tribe vary greatly, there is enough textual evidence to support the claim that we have two versions of the same basic blessing.

In Jacob's blessing, we have *"Judah is a lion's whelp"* (Gen. 49:9); in Moses' blessing, we have *"And of Dan he said, Dan is a lion's whelp"* (Deut. 33:22). More striking, however, are the blessings given to Joseph:

> *The blessings of thy father have prevailed above the blessings of my progenitors unto the utmost bound of the everlasting hills: they shall be on the head of Joseph, and on the crown of the head of him that was separate from his brethren* (Gen. 49:26).

> *And of Joseph he said, Blessed of the Lord be his land. . . . And for the chief things of the ancient mountains, and for the precious things of the lasting hills . . . let the blessing come upon the head of Joseph, and upon the top of the head of him that was separated from his brethren* (Deut. 33:13, 15, 16).

It is certainly possible that both Jacob and Moses might have used the same words in blessing Joseph, but it is more likely that we have two distinct versions of the same basic blessing.

As for the names of the twelve tribes, we have an earlier version in Genesis, in which the order of names appears to be determined in part because some of the sons of Jacob were born not from his wives Leah and Rachel but rather from their handmaids Bilhah and Zilpah:

> *Now the sons of Jacob were twelve: The sons of Leah; Reuben, Jacob's firstborn, and Simeon, and Levi, and Judah, and Issachar, and Zebulun; The sons of Rachel: Joseph, and Benjamin; And the sons of Bilhah, Rachel's handmaid: Dan, and Naphtali; and the sons of Zilpah, Leah's handmaid: Gad, and Asher. These are the sons of Jacob* (Gen. 35:22–26).

As for further variation in the list of the names of the twelve tribes, we have additional versions of the list in the first chapter of Numbers and the second chapter of 1 Chronicles, plus another version in Revelation, the very last book of the Bible. The list in Numbers (1:5–15) has only eleven names—presumably the missing name is Levi—but the lists in 1 Chronicles (2:1–2) and Revelation (7:5–8) have twelve.

Numbers List	Chronicles List	Revelation List
Reuben	Reuben	Juda
Simeon	Simeon	Reuben
Judah	Levi	Gad
Issachar	Judah	Aser
Zebulun	Issachar	Nephthalim
Joseph	Zebulun	Manasses
Benjamin	Dan	Simeon
Dan	Joseph	Levi
Asher	Benjamin	Issachar
Gad	Naphtali	Zabulon
Naphtali	Gad	Joseph
	Asher	Benjamin

Comparing these third, fourth, and fifth versions with the other two, we note that Dan, which is found on both Jacob's and Moses' lists, is included on the Numbers and Chronicles lists but is missing from the Revelation list. However, Simeon, which was on Jacob's list, is also found in the Numbers, Chronicles, and Revelation lists. On the other hand, the Revelation list included Manasses as one of the twelve tribes, a name that appears on none of the other four lists. (Manasseh is listed in Numbers 1:10, but only as one of the children of Joseph, not as a separate tribe. In the book of Joshua, however, Manasseh is referred to in one passage as a tribe (17:1) and in another as a half tribe (13:29).) If we combine all the names of the twelve tribes of Israel on the five lists, we have a total of fourteen names. Nine of the names are found on all five lists, but the other five are not. There are four occurrences of Dan, four occurrences of Simeon, four occurrences of Levi, and one occurrence each of Jeshurun and Manasses. This may pose a problem for the historian seeking to know the identity of the twelve tribes of Israel, but not for the folklorist who understands the nature of oral tradition and who is not surprised by its inevitable variation.

It may come as a bit of a shock to come to learn that there are also differences with respect to the names and identities of the twelve apostles. One might have thought that at least on this issue there would be total consensus. Let us compare the various lists of the disciples:

> *Now the names of the twelve apostles are these: The first, Simon, who is called Peter, and Andrew his brother; James the son of Zebedee, and John his brother; Philip and Bartholomew; Thomas and Matthew the publican; James the son of Alpheus, and Lebbeus, whose surname was **Thaddeus**; Simon the Canaanite, and Judas Iscariot, who also betrayed him* (Matt. 10:2–4).

Mark's list of names is virtually identical, although the order differs:

> *And he ordained twelve . . . Simon he surnamed Peter; and James the son of Zebedee, and John the brother of James; and he surnamed them Boanerges, which is the sons of thunder; and Andrew and Philip and Bartholomew, and Matthew, and Thomas, and James the son of Alpheus, and **Thaddeus**, and Simon the Canaanite, and Judas Iscariot, which also betrayed him* (Mark 3:14, 16–19).

But Luke's list is not identical:

And when it was day, he called unto him his disciples: and of them he chose
twelve, whom also he named apostles: Simon (whom he also named Peter),
and Andrew his brother, James and John, Philip and Bartholomew, Mat-
thew and Thomas, James the son of Alpheus, and Simon called Zelotes, and
Judas the brother of James, *and Judas Iscariot, which also was the traitor*
(Luke 6:13–16).

The name of Thaddeus is not on Luke's list, but the name of another
Judas, this one being the brother of James, is! Is this merely scribal
error? Consider the list given in Acts:

And when they were come in, they went up into an upper room where
abode both Peter and James, and John, and Andrew, Philip, and Thomas,
Bartholomew, and Matthew, James the son of Alpheus, and Simon Zelotes,
and ***Judas, the brother of James*** (Acts 1:13).

This last list does not include Judas Iscariot since this assembly took
place after the crucifixion, although he is mentioned as one who had
been *"numbered with us and had obtained part of this ministry"* (Acts
1:17). This suggests that Judas the brother of James is not the same as
Judas Iscariot. There is also the evidence from John (14:22) that reads:
"Judas saith unto him [Jesus], *not Iscariot. . . ."* This would also indicate
that one of the disciples was named Judas and further that he was not
to be confused with Judas Iscariot. Again, the name of Thaddeus is
missing from the list in Acts. So two lists, those of Matthew and Mark,
include Thaddeus but make no mention of Judas the brother of James;
two lists, those of Luke and Acts, include Judas the brother of James
but make no mention of Thaddeus. One might surmise therefore that
there are two separate traditional lists of the twelve apostles and that
these two lists are not verbatim identical.

As there are important differences in the names of individuals in the
Bible, there are also significant variations in the names of places, especially places that figure prominently in religious history. For example,
Jesus, after having bade a final farewell to his faithful disciples, is said
to have ascended to heaven. The question is, What was the name of the
place from which Jesus began his ascent? In one version, it is Bethany.

And he led them out as far as to ***Bethany,*** *and he lifted up his hands,*
and blessed them. And it came to pass, while he blessed them, he was parted
from them, and carried up into heaven (Luke 24:50–51).

And when he had spoken these things, while they beheld, he was taken up; and a cloud received him out of their sight. . . . Then returned they unto Jerusalem from the mount called Olivet, which is from Jerusalem a sabbath day's journey (Acts 1:9, 12).

If Acts was in fact written by Luke, it is curious that he recorded both versions of the ascension, one from the Mount of Olives and one from Bethany.

Another illustration of the variations in place-names found in multiple versions of the same event is found in accounts of where individuals were buried. Take the case of Moses' brother Aaron. There are two versions of his death and burial. In one, God instructs Moses: "*Take Aaron and Eleazar his son and bring them up unto mount Hor*" which was "*by the coast of the land of Edom*" (Num. 20:20, 25). Moses obeyed God "*And Moses stripped Aaron of his garments, and put them upon Eleazar his son; and Aaron died there in the top of the mount*" (Num. 20:28). But in a second version, a different burial place is mentioned. "*And the children of Israel took their journey from Beeroth of the children of Jaakan to Mosera: there Aaron died, and there he was buried; and Eleazar his son ministered in the priest's office in his stead*" (Deut. 10:6).

Even more puzzling are the details surrounding the accounts describing where Jacob was buried. The critical question is, Who purchased the burial plot and from whom was it purchased? According to Genesis 50:13, "*And his [Jacob's] sons carried him into the land of Canaan, and buried him in the cave of the field of Machpelah, which Abraham bought with the field for a possession of a burying place of Ephron the Hittite, before Mamre.*" This seems straightforward enough. Jacob was buried in a cave on a plot purchased by Abraham from Ephron the Hittite. However, Acts 7:15–16 reports, "*So Jacob went down into Egypt, and died, he, and our fathers, And were carried over into Sychem, and laid in the sepulchre that Abraham bought for a sum of money of the sons of Emmor, the father of Sychem.*" Abraham is still listed as the purchaser of the burial plot, but the seller is no longer Ephron the Hittite, but rather the sons of Emmor, the father of Sychem. This reminds us of the account in Joshua 24:32, in which it is reported "*And the bones of Joseph, which the children of Israel brought up out of Egypt, buried they in Shechem, in a parcel of ground which Jacob bought of the sons of Hammor the father of Shechem for a hundred pieces of silver; and it became the inheritance of the children of Joseph.*" This account clearly is related to the one in Acts; Hammor and Emmor surely are variants of the same name. But while the seller of the burial plot is the same, the purchaser in this case is not Abraham but Jacob. Now one might well ask if it really matters at this point who did purchase the burial plot, Abraham or Jacob. Probably not, but the point is that with multiple oral versions of the same event, one would normally expect to find variation, and that is precisely what one does find.

Speaking of Jacob, we are reminded that just as personal names may vary in different versions of a particular incident, so can place-names. Jacob's name is changed by God to Israel, and the question is, What was the name of the place where this momentous name change occurred? In the first version of this onomastic occasion, Jacob wrestles with a stranger and refuses to release him until his opponent blesses him:

> And he said unto him, What is thy name? And he said, Jacob. And he said, Thy name shall be called no more Jacob, but Israel: for as a prince hast thou power with God and with men, and hast prevailed. . . . And Jacob called the name of the place **Peniel**: for I have seen God face to face, and my life is preserved (Gen. 32:27–28, 30).

But in a second version of the divine name-changing legend, the locale appears to be a different one:

> And God appeared unto Jacob again, when he came out of **Padanaram**, and blessed him. And God said unto him, Thy name is Jacob: thy name shall not be called any more Jacob, but Israel shall be thy name; and he called his name Israel (Gen. 35:9–10).

Again, one might remonstrate: does it really matter where Jacob is renamed Israel? Probably not, but it does show that we have two different versions of the same story, which makes it a case of folklore.

Incidentally, Jacob's claim that he had seen God "face to face" reminds us of the debate over whether a man could or could not see the face of God. In Exodus, Moses was specifically forbidden to look upon God's face: "*And he said, Thou canst not see my face: for there shall no man see me, and live*" (Exod. 33:20). Still, we are also told immediately after this passage, "*And the Lord said, Behold, there is a place by me, and thou shalt stand upon a rock: And it shall come to pass, while my glory passeth by, that I will put thee in a cleft of the rock, and will cover thee with my hand while I pass by: And I will take away mine hand, and thou shalt see my back parts; but my face shall not be seen*" (Exod. 33:21–23).

Evidently God in this instance did permit Moses to see his "back parts" but not his face. On the other hand, earlier in Exodus, we learn: "*And the Lord spake unto Moses face to face, as a man speaketh unto his friend*" (Exod. 33:11). This face-to-face encounter is apparently confirmed by one of the last lines of Deuteronomy, a book of the Bible supposedly written by Moses himself: "*And there arose not a prophet since in Israel like unto Moses, whom the Lord knew face to face*" (Deut. 34:10). If both Jacob and Moses did see God face to face, this might call into question the unequivocal statement in the New Testament: "*No man hath seen God at any time*" (John 1:18).

Variation in Sequence

So far we have demonstrated variation in numbers and names, but there is also variation in sequence. Two versions of the same story may contain similar content presented in a different order or sequence. The very first lines of Genesis provide an example: "*In the beginning God created the **heaven** and the **earth**"* (Gen. 1:1). The order of creation, as indicated in this opening line, is heaven first, earth second. But compare another version in the second chapter of Genesis: "*In the day that the Lord God made the **earth** and the **heavens**"* (Gen. 2:4). Here the order is reversed: earth first, heaven second. By itself, this variation in word order might be considered trivial, a mere stylistic inconsistency, but as we shall soon see, placed in the context of countless other duplicate texts or versions, we can discern a similar pattern throughout the Old and New Testaments.

It may be instructive to look at two versions of another creation myth in Genesis. In this instance, the topic is the creation of animals and whether they are created before or after the first man:

> *And God made the beast of the earth after his kind, and cattle, after their kind and every thing that creepeth upon the earth after his kind: and God saw that it was good. And God said, Let us make man in our image. . . . So God created man in his own image* (Gen. 1:25–27).

The sequence is clear. First animals are created and then man. But we get a different version in the very next chapter of Genesis:

> *And the Lord God formed man of the dust of ground, and breathed into his nostrils the breath of life; and man became a living soul. . . . And the Lord*

God said, It is not good that man should be alone; I will make a help meet for him. And out of the ground the Lord God formed every beast of the field, and every fowl of the air; and brought them unto Adam to see what he would call them: and whatsoever Adam called every living creature, that was the name thereof (Gen. 2:7, 18–19).

Here the sequence is also very clear. First man is created and then the other animals. From a feminist perspective, sequence is more of an issue in the two versions of the creation of woman. We may distinguish the two versions by calling the first "simultaneous creation" and the second "sequential creation." The first chapter of Genesis contains the first version:

So God created man in his own image, in the image of God created he him; male and female created he them (Gen. 1:27).

Now it is true that "male" is mentioned before "female," but essentially we have a simultaneous creation of man and woman. The second version is more blatantly chauvinistic inasmuch as normal biological reality is reversed. Instead of man being born from woman's body, woman is born from man's body.

And the Lord God caused a deep sleep to fall upon Adam, and he slept; and he took one of his ribs, and closed up the flesh instead thereof. And the rib, which the Lord God had taken from man, made he a woman, and brought her unto the man (Gen. 2:22).

The sequence is: first man is created and then later, only after all the other animals are created, woman is created.

Some of the other sequential variation in the Old Testament is much less significant, but it qualifies as variation nonetheless. For example, there are two versions of the banishing of Sarah's handmaid, Hagar. In this incident, Sarah has difficulty conceiving and presents Hagar to her husband, Abraham, so that she, Sarah, *"may obtain children by her"* (Gen. 16:2). In the first version, after Hagar becomes pregnant, Sarah feels that Hagar despises her and asks Abraham to dismiss Hagar. Abraham agrees to let Sarah do as she wishes in the matter. *"And when Sarai dealt hardly with her, she* [Hagar] *fled from her face"* (Gen. 16:6). But God sends an angel to look after Hagar:

And the angel of the Lord found her by a fountain of water in the wilderness. . . . And the angel of the Lord said unto her, I will multiply thy seed exceedingly that it shall not be numbered for multitude. And the angel of the Lord said unto her, Behold, thou art with child, and shalt bear a son, and shalt call his name Ishmael; because the Lord hath heard thy affliction. And he will be a wild man. . . . Wherefore the well was called Beerlahairoi. . . . And Hagar bare Abram a son: and Abram called his son's name, which Hagar bare, Ishmael (Gen. 16:7, 10–12, 14, 15).

In the second version of Hagar's banishment, she gives birth to Ishmael **before** being sent away:

And Sarah saw the son of Hagar the Egyptian, which she had borne unto Abraham, mocking. Wherefore she said unto Abraham, Cast out this bond-woman and her son: for the son of this bondwoman shall not be heir with my son, even with Isaac. . . . And God said unto Abraham, Let it not be grievous in thy sight because of the lad, and because of thy bondwoman; in all that Sarah hath said unto thee, hearken unto her voice; for in Isaac shall thy seed by called. And also of the son of the bondwoman will I make a nation, because he is thy seed. And Abraham rose up early in the morning, and took bread, and a bottle of water, and gave it to Hagar, putting it on her shoulder, and the child, and sent her away: and she departed, and wandered in the wilderness of Beersheba. And the water was spent in the bottle, and she cast the child under one of the shrubs. . . . she said, Let me not see the death of the child. . . . And God heard the voice of the lad and the angel of God called to Hagar out of heaven. . . . Arise, lift up the lad, and hold him in thine hand; for I will make him a great nation. And God opened her eyes, she saw a well of water; and she went, and filled the bottle with water, and gave the lad drink. And God was with the lad; and he grew, and dwelt in the wilderness, and became an archer (Gen. 21:9–15, 17, 18–20).

The sequential issue is whether Hagar gave birth to Ishmael **before** or **after** being banished.

Another relatively minor instance of sequential variation has to do with King Josiah. He was evidently mortally wounded in a battle at Megiddo and was eventually buried in Jerusalem. The question is, Did he die at Megiddo **before** or **after** being transported by chariot to Jerusalem? Here are two versions of the event:

*In his days Pharaoh-nechoh king of Egypt went up against the king of Assyria to the river Euphrates: and king Josiah went against him; and he slew him at Megiddo, when he had seen him. And his servants carried him in a chariot **dead from Megiddo, and brought him to Jerusalem,** and buried him in his own sepulchre* (2 Kings 23:29–30).

> *After all this, when Josiah had prepared the temple, Necho king of Egypt came up to fight against Carchemish by Euphrates: and Josiah went out against him . . . and came to fight in the valley of Megiddo. And the archers shot at king Josiah; and the king said to his servants, Have me away; for I am sore wounded. His servants therefore took him out of that chariot, and put him in the second chariot that he had; **and they brought him to Jerusalem, and he died,** and was buried in one of the sepulchres of his fathers* (2 Chron. 35:20, 22–24).

There is agreement that Josiah died as a result of wounds inflicted at Megiddo, but it is not clear whether he died at Megiddo and his corpse carried to Jerusalem for burial or whether he was wounded at Megiddo and carried to Jerusalem, where he died and was subsequently buried. Does it really matter? Perhaps not, but it does constitute another instructive example of what happens when there are conflicting oral traditions supposedly describing the same historical event.

There are sequential disparities in the New Testament as well, perhaps not as serious as those in the creation myths in Genesis. Several instances should suffice. One of these concerns Bethlehem, the alleged birthplace of Jesus, and the town of Nazareth. According to Matthew, *"Jesus was born in Bethlehem of Judea in the days of Herod the king"* (2:1). Then an *"angel of the Lord appeareth to Joseph in a dream, saying, Arise, and take the young child and his mother, and flee into Egypt"* (2:13). *"But when Herod was dead, behold, an angel of the Lord appeared in a dream to Joseph in Egypt, Saying, Arise, and take the young child and his mother, and go into the land of Israel. . . . And he came and dwelt in a city called Nazareth: that it might be fulfilled, which was spoken by the prophets, He shall be called a Nazarene"* (2:19, 23). So the sequence is explicit: From Bethlehem to Egypt to Nazareth. In this version, there is no indication that Joseph had previously lived in Nazareth. In Luke's version, however, the story begins in Nazareth. *"And in the sixth month the angel Gabriel was sent from God unto a city of Galilee, named Nazareth, To a virgin espoused to a man whose name was Joseph"* (1:26–27). And then in order to be taxed, Joseph took his pregnant wife from Nazareth to Bethlehem. *"And Joseph also went up from Galilee, out of the city of Nazareth, into Judea, unto the city of David, which is called Bethlehem"* (2:4). After Jesus was born in Bethlehem and circumcised, Joseph and Mary brought him to Jerusalem *"to present him to the Lord"* (2:22). *"And when they had performed all things according to the law of the Lord, they returned into Galilee, to their own city Nazareth"*

(2:39). So the sequence in Luke is: Nazareth, Bethlehem, Jerusalem, Nazareth. In Luke's version, there is no mention at all of the "flight into Egypt," and Nazareth is said to be Joseph's hometown. In terms of sequence, we have Matthew's move from Bethlehem to Nazareth (via Egypt) and we have Luke's move from Nazareth to Bethlehem back to Nazareth (via Jerusalem).

An even more obvious illustration of sequential variation in the New Testament is provided by the different versions of the temptations of Christ. The devil seeks to test Jesus in a series of three temptations that include asking him to turn stones into bread, to jump down from the pinnacle of the temple to be caught by angels, and to accept dominion over all the kingdoms of the world. Compare the accounts in Matthew and Luke:

Then was Jesus led up of the Spirit into the wilderness to be tempted of the devil. And when he had fasted forty days and forty nights, he was afterward ahungered. And when the tempter came to him, he said, If thou be the Son of God, command that these stones be made bread. But he answered and said, It is written, Man shall not live by bread alone, but by every word that proceedeth out of the mouth of God. Then the devil taketh him up into the holy city, and setteth him on a pinnacle of the temple. And saith unto him, If thou be the Son of God, cast thyself down; for it is written, He shall give his angels charge concerning thee: and in their hands they shall bear thee up, lest at any time thou dash thy foot against a stone. Jesus said unto him, It is written again, Thou shalt not tempt the Lord thy God. Again, the devil taketh him up into an exceeding high mountain, and showing him all the kingdoms of the world, and the glory of them; And saith unto him, All these things will I give thee, if thou wilt fall down and worship me. Then saith Jesus unto him. Get thee hence, Satan: for it is written, Thou shalt worship the Lord thy God, and him only shalt thou serve. Then the devil leaveth him, and behold angels came and ministered unto him (Matt. 4:1–11).

Luke offers a slightly different version of the three temptations:

And Jesus being full of the Holy Ghost returned from Jordan, and was led by the Spirit into the wilderness. Being forty days tempted of the devil, And in those days he did eat nothing: and when they were ended, he afterward hungered. And the devil said unto him, If thou be the Son of God, command this stone that it be made bread. And Jesus answered him, saying, It is written, That man shall not live by bread alone, but by every word of God. and the devil, taking him into a high mountain, showed unto him all the kingdoms of the world in a moment of time. And the devil said unto

him, All this power will I give thee, and the glory of them: for that is deliv-
ered unto me; and to whomsoever I will, I give it. If thou therefore wilt wor-
ship me, all shall be thine. And Jesus answered and said unto him, Get thee
behind me Satan: for it is written, Thou shalt worship the Lord thy God,
and him only shalt thou serve. And he brought him to Jerusalem and set
him on a pinnacle of the temple, and said unto him, If thou be the Son of
God, cast thyself down from hence: For it is written, He shall give his angels
charge over thee, to keep thee: And in their hands they shall bear thee up,
lest any time thou dash thy foot against a stone. And Jesus answering said
unto him. It is said, Thou shalt not tempt the Lord thy God. And when the
devil had ended all the temptation, he departed from him for a season
(Luke 4:1–13).

There is a numerical variation—plural stones to be made into bread
in Matthew versus a single stone in Luke—but surely the more significant variation involves sequence. For Matthew, the pinnacle jump is
temptation number two with the dominion offer constituting the third
and final temptation. For Luke, this order is reversed, with the dominion coming second and the pinnacle third. One could argue, I suppose,
that the order of temptations is not really very important, but from the
perspective of historical accuracy it is unlikely that **both** sequences can
be deemed chronologically correct.

The devil also figures in another clear example of sequential variation. Evidently, Satan entered the body of Judas Iscariot so that Judas
would betray Jesus. The sequential issue turns on whether Satan entered Judas **before** or **after** the Last Supper. According to Luke, Satan
enters into Judas well before the Last Supper:

> *Now the feast of unleavened bread drew nigh, which is called the Pass-*
> *over. And the chief priests and scribes sought how they might kill him; for*
> *they feared the people. **Then entered Satan into Judas** surnamed Iscariot,*
> *being of the number of the twelve. And he went his way, and communed*
> *with the chief priests and captains, how he might betray him unto them.*
> *. . . **Then came the day of unleavened bread.** . . .* (Luke 22:1–4, 7).

However, John provides not one but two different versions of the same
incident. In one version, Jesus is asked which of the disciples will betray
him. His response:

> *Jesus answered, He it is, to whom I shall give a sop, when I have dipped*
> *it. And when he had dipped the sop, he gave it to Judas Iscariot, the son of*
> *Simon. **And after the sop Satan entered into him** (John 13:26–27).*

This would suggest that Satan entered into Judas during the Last Supper. Matthew and Mark in their versions of Jesus' answer to the same question also indicate that this action takes place during the meal. In their versions, however, Jesus does not hand Judas a sop. Instead, Judas is said to dip his own sop in the dish of Jesus:

> *And he answered and said, He that dippeth his hand with me in the dish, the same shall betray me* (Matt. 26:23).

> *And he answered and said unto them, It is one of the twelve, that dippeth with me in the dish* (Mark 14:20).

In a second version reported by John, we find the suggestion that Satan entered Judas after the meal:

> *And supper being ended, the devil having now put into the heart of Judas Iscariot, Simon's son, to betray him* (John 13:2).

So the question is: did Satan enter into Judas before, during, or after the Last Supper? Satan's culpability is not at all in doubt, but the sequence of his actions is.

Another instance of sequential variation occurs in an event involving John the Baptist. It is the celebrated episode in which John the Baptist predicts the coming of one greater than he. We may begin with Matthew's version:

> *I indeed baptize you with water unto repentance: but he that cometh after me is mightier than I, whose shoes I am not worthy to bear: he shall baptize you with the Holy Ghost, and with fire* (Matt. 3:11).

In this version, we have a reference to water baptism, followed by a shoe comparison, and ending with an evidently superior baptism involving the Holy Ghost. Luke's version displays the same sequence:

> *John answered, saying unto them all, I indeed baptize you with water; but one mightier than I cometh, the latchet of whose shoes I am not worthy to unloose: he shall baptize you with the Holy Ghost and with fire* (Luke 3:16).

John's version follows the same order but with slightly different wording:

> *John answered them, saying, I baptize with water: but there standeth one*
> *among you, whom ye know not; He it is, who coming after me is preferred*
> *before me, whose shoe-latches I am not worthy to unloose . . . the same is*
> *he which baptizeth with the Holy Ghost* (John 1:26–27, 33).

Mark's version, however, presents a different sequence:

> *And* [John] *preached saying, There cometh one mightier than I after me,*
> *the latchet of whose shoes I am not worthy to stoop down and unloose. I*
> *indeed have baptized you with water: but he shall baptize you with the Holy*
> *Ghost* (Mark 1:7–8).

Mark's order is: shoe comparison, water baptism, and Holy Ghost baptism. It is perhaps a small variation, but it is nevertheless a definite difference in sequential structure.

Let me give another illustration of obvious sequential variation. The question revolves around whether Jesus threw out the money changers from the temple **before** or **after** he cursed a certain barren fig tree. According to Matthew:

> *And Jesus went into the temple of God, and cast out all of them that sold*
> *and bought in the temple, and overthrew the tables of the money changers,*
> *and the seats of them that sold doves.* [And then after leaving the area
> Jesus went to Bethany where next morning he was hungry.] *And when*
> *he saw a fig tree in the way, he came to it, and found nothing thereon, but*
> *leaves only, and said unto it, Let no fruit grow on thee henceforward for*
> *ever. And presently the fig tree withered away* (21:12, 19).

Mark describes the same two incidents but presents them in a different order:

> *And on the morrow, when they were come from Bethany, he was hungry:*
> *And seeing a fig tree afar off having leaves, he came, if haply he might find*
> *any thing thereon: and when he came to it, he found nothing but leaves; for*
> *the time of figs was not yet. And Jesus answered and said unto it, No man*
> *eat fruit of thee hereafter for ever. And his disciples heard it. and they came*
> *to Jerusalem and Jesus went into the temple, and began to cast out them*
> *that sold and bought in the temple, and overthrew the tables of the money*
> *changers, and the seats of them that sold doves* (11:12–15).

In connection with this illustration of sequential variation, it is also worth remarking on the amount of time required for the fig tree to wither away. In Matthew's version, the tree is affected by Jesus' curse almost immediately. Indeed, the disciples even comment on the speed with which the curse takes effect:

> *And presently the fig tree withered away. And when the disciples saw it, they marveled, saying, How soon is the fig tree withered away!* (Matt. 21:19–20)

In contrast, Mark's account suggests that the disciples did not notice the dried-up fig tree until the next morning:

> *And in the morning, as they passed by, they saw the fig tree dried up from the roots. And Peter calling to remembrance saith unto him, Master, behold, the fig tree which thou cursedst is withered away* (Mark 11:20–21).

Another curious illustration of sequential variation concerns whether the soldiers placed a crown of thorns on the head of Jesus before or after they put a robe on him. According to one version, Jesus was robed before being crowned:

> *Then the soldiers of the governor took Jesus into the common hall, and gathered unto him the whole band of soldiers. And they stripped him, and put on him a scarlet robe. And when they had platted a crown of thorns, they put it upon his head* (Matthew 27:27–29).

But in another version, he is crowned before being robed:

> *And the soldiers platted a crown of thorns, and put it on his head, and they put on him a purple robe* (John 19:2).

A third version contains elements of both these accounts. As in the first version, the robe comes before the crown, but the color of the robe is not scarlet but rather is purple as it is in the second version.

> *And they clothed him with purple and platted a crown of thorns, and put it above his head* (Mark 15:17).

In the present context, it may be useful to compare two versions of Paul's famous conversion on the way to Damascus. The first account is third-person reportorial, whereas the second version is narrated in the first person. With respect to sequence, the issue is whether the men accompanying Paul are described **before** or **after** Paul asks Jesus for instructions as to what to do or where to go.

> *And as he journeyed, he came near Damascus: and suddenly there shined round about him a light from heaven: And he fell to the earth, and heard a voice saying unto him, Saul, Saul, why persecutest thou me? And he said, Who are thou, Lord? And the Lord said, I am Jesus whom thou persecutest: it is hard for thee to kick against the pricks. And he trembling and astonished said, Lord, what wilt thou have me to do? And the Lord said unto him, Arise, and go into the city, and it shall be told thee what thou must do. And the men which journeyed with him stood speechless, **hearing a voice** but seeing no man. And Saul arose from the earth; and when his eyes were opened, he saw no man: but they led him by the hand, and brought him into Damascus* (Acts 9:3–8).

Here is the first-person account:

> *And it came to pass, that, as I made my journey, and was come nigh unto Damascus about noon, suddenly there shone from heaven a great light round about me. And I fell unto the ground, and heard a voice saying unto me, Saul, Saul, why persecutest thou me? And I answered, Who are thou, Lord? And he said unto me, I am Jesus of Nazareth, whom thou persecutest. And they that were with me saw indeed the light, and were afraid: but they **heard not the voice** of him that spake to me. And I said, What shall I do, Lord? And the Lord said unto me, Arise, and go into Damascus; and there it shall be told thee of all things which are appointed for thee to do. And when I could not see for the glory of that light, being led by the hand of them that were with me, I came into Damascus* (Acts 22:6–11).

These are pretty similar accounts, but there are slight differences in wording. Jesus in the first version becomes Jesus of Nazareth in the second. Another difference occurs regarding sequence. In the first version the men accompanying Paul are described **after** Paul asks Jesus for instruction. In the second version the men are described **before** Paul requests instruction. Even more striking is the disparity between the descriptions of what the accompanying men observed. In the first version, the men stood speechless, hearing a voice; in the second version, the men "*heard not the voice of him that spake.*" Presumably the men either did or did not hear a voice. Two versions, two different accounts!

In yet a third version, it is not completely clear whether the men did or did not hear a voice. Paul reports only that he heard the voice: "*And when we were all fallen to the earth I heard a voice speaking unto me, and saying in the Hebrew tongue, Saul, Saul, why persecutest thou me? it is hard for thee to kick against the pricks"* (Acts 26:14). So the implication is perhaps that the men with him did **not** hear the voice. But we do have the additional detail in this third version that the voice spoke in Hebrew, a detail not contained in the first two versions.

More Duplicate Texts

After demonstrating how number, name, and sequence vary from version to version, as is common in oral tradition, I should now like to review a generous sampling of duplicate passages in both the Old and New Testaments to show just how pervasive such multiforms are. There are so many that it would take a book nearly as long as the Bible itself to document them all. I also intend to make good my claim that nearly all of the most celebrated and significant portions of the Bible exist in at least two versions.

I want to remind the reader that when I refer to duplicate texts, that does not mean that they are verbatim identical, although in numerous instances they are close to that. Consider, for example, Psalm 14 and Psalm 53. Even the most skeptical critic could not possibly read these two texts and fail to acknowledge that they are the same song. Most of the lines are nearly exactly the same, word for word. Still, there is one passage that does demonstrate variation:

> *There were they in great fear: for God is in the generation of the righteous. Ye have shamed the counsel of the poor, because the Lord is his refuge* (Ps. 14:5–6).

> *There were they in great fear, where no fear was: for God hath scattered the bones of him that encampeth against thee: thou has put them to shame, because God hath despised them* (Ps. 53:5).

In the same way, one can compare the short Psalm 70 with Psalm 40:13–17:

> *Make haste, O God, to deliver me; make haste to help me, Let them be ashamed and confounded that seek after my soul: let them be turned back-*

ward, and put to confusion that desire my hurt. Let them be turned back for a reward of their shame that say, Aha, aha. Let all those that seek thee rejoice and be glad in thee: and let such as love thy salvation say continually, Let God be magnified. But I am poor and needy; make haste unto me, O God; thou art my help and my deliverer; O Lord, make no tarrying (Psalm 70).

Be pleased, O Lord, to deliver me: O Lord, make haste to help me. Let them be ashamed and confounded together that seek after my soul to destroy it; let them be driven backward and put to shame that wish me evil. Let them be desolate for a reward of their shame that say unto me, Aha, aha. Let all those that seek thee rejoice and be glad in thee: let such as love thy salvation say continually, The Lord be magnified. But I am poor and needy; yet the Lord thinketh upon me: thou art my help and my deliverer: make no tarrying, O my God (Psalm 90:13–17).

There are parallels to passages in the psalms elsewhere in the Bible. For example, one may compare 2 Samuel 22 with Psalm 18. In both texts, David is singing a song to thank God for having delivered him from the hands of his enemies. Here are the initial lines of the two passages:

And he said, The Lord is my rock, and my fortress, and my deliverer, The God of my rock; in him will I trust: he is my shield, and the horn of my salvation, my high tower, and my refuge, my saviour; thou savest me from violence (2 Sam. 22:2–3).

The Lord is my rock, and my fortress, and my deliverer; my God my strength, in whom I will trust; my buckler, and the horn of my salvation, and my high tower (Ps. 18:2).

Although many lines in the two passages are virtually identical, there are other parallel lines that reflect the same degree of variation found in these initial lines. Here is one example:

Thou has also given me the shield of thy salvation: and thy gentleness hath made me great (2 Sam. 22:36).

*Thou hast also given me the shield of thy salvation: **and thy right hand hath holden me up,** and thy gentleness hath made me great* (Ps. 18:35).

There is obviously a phrase in the Psalm 18 version that is not found in the 2 Samuel 22 version. Whether the Psalm version is the original and the Samuel version simply lost the phrase in question or the Samuel version is the original and the Psalm version simply added the phrase in question is not the issue. What is significant is that we have two versions of the same song and there is variation, an unmistakable clue that we are dealing with folklore. This particular set of passages, along with others, was ably discussed by Ringgren some years ago, and he understood very well that such apparent discrepancies in duplicate passages might be attributable to original oral transmission (1950–51:39–45). However, he did not consider the entire Old Testament, and he did not look at the New Testament at all from this perspective.

Another example of duplicate texts that contain definite variation involves passages from Matthew and James:

> *But I say unto you, Swear not at all; neither by heaven; for it is God's throne: Nor by the earth; for it is his footstool. . . . But let your communication be, Yea, yea; Nay, nay; for whatsoever is more than these cometh of evil* (Matt. 5:34–35, 37).

> *But above all things, my brethren, swear not, neither by heaven, neither by the earth, neither by any other oath: but let your yea be yea; and your nay, nay; lest ye fall into condemnation* (James 5:12).

How individuals die or are killed provides numerous illustrations of multiple existence and variation. There are two versions relating how a brave woman killed an enemy general. Consider the following two accounts of Jael's dispatching of Sisera, who, in flight after his troops' defeat, sought refuge in her tent:

> *Howbeit Sisera fled away on his feet to the tent of Jael the wife of Heber the Kenite: for there was peace between Jabin the king of Hazor and the house of Heber the Kenite. And Jael went out to meet Sisera, and said unto him, Turn in, my lord, turn in to me; fear not. And when he had turned in unto her in the tent, she covered him with a mantle. And he said unto her, Give me, I pray thee, a little water to drink; for I am thirsty. And she opened a bottle of milk, and gave him drink, and covered him. Again he said unto her, Stand in the door of the tent, and it shall be, when any man doth come and inquire of thee, and say, Is there any man here? that thou shalt say, No. Then Jael Heber's wife took a nail of the tent, and took a hammer in*

her hand, and went softly unto him, and **smote the nail into his temples,** *and fastened it to the ground: for he was fast asleep and weary. So he died* (Judg. 4:17–21).

The second account is much briefer, but it contains details not found in the first account:

> *Blessed above women shall Jael the wife of Heber the Kenite be: blessed shall she be above women in the tent. He asked water, and she gave him milk; she brought forth butter in a lordly dish. She put her hand to the nail, and her right hand to the workmen's hammer; and with the hammer she smote Sisera,* **she smote off his head, when she had pierced and stricken through his temples.** *At her feet he bowed, he fell, he lay down: at her feet he bowed, he fell: where he bowed, there he fell down dead* (Judg. 5:24–27).

That Jael killed Sisera in her tent is not in dispute, but there are significant variations as to how she accomplished this. In the first account, Sisera was evidently lying down asleep when Jael attacked him with a hammer and nail. In addition to offering him a drink, she covered him with a blanket or mantle before killing him. In the second account, there is no mention of Sisera's reclining position, and she seems to have decapitated him (*"smote off his head"*). In any case, Sisera is specifically said to have fallen down in the second account, which could not have happened if he had been killed in his sleep as described in the first account. What we have once again are two different versions of the same event. The telltale sign of orality is also signaled by the poetic repetition as a finale: *"**At her feet he bowed, he fell,** he lay down: **at her feet he bowed, he fell:** where he bowed, there he fell down dead"* (Judg. 5:27).

Another contrasting set of versions describing the death of an individual is found in the Old Testament. In the struggle for power between David and Saul, Saul is eventually killed in a battle. Here are the two versions:

> *And the battle went sore against Saul, and the archers hit him; and he was sore wounded of the archers. Then said Saul unto his armor-bearer, Draw thy sword, and thrust me through therewith; lest these uncircumcised come and thrust me through, and abuse me. But his armor-bearer would not; for he was sore afraid.* **Therefore Saul took a sword, and fell upon it.** *And when his armor-bearer saw that Saul was dead, he fell likewise upon his sword, and died with him. So Saul died* (1 Sam. 31:3–6).

From this account, we gather that Saul decided that rather than dying at the hand of the Philistines, he would take his own life. In a second version, however, Saul does **not** take his own life. And it is not his armor bearer or a Philistine who kills him. Rather it is a young Amalekite, who reports to David that he killed Saul.

And David said unto the young man that told him, How knowest thou that Saul and Jonathan his son be dead? And the young man that told him said, As I happened by chance upon mount Gilboa, behold, Saul leaned upon his spear; and, lo, the chariots and horsemen followed hard after him. . . . And he said unto me, Who art thou? And I answered him, I am an Amalekite. **He said** *unto me again, Stand, I pray thee, upon me, and* **slay me:** *for anguish is come upon me, because my life is yet whole in me.* **So I stood upon him, and slew him,** *because I was sure that he could not live after that he was fallen: and I took the crown that was upon his head, and the bracelet that was on his arm, and have brought them hither unto my lord* (2 Sam. 1:5–6, 8–10).

The question of whether Saul died by his own hand on the battle-field or whether he asked a passing Amalekite youth to slay him and the latter did so remains unresolved. The fact that Saul was killed is not in dispute, but just how he died is.

While on the subject of Saul and David, we might comment briefly on the divergent accounts of how these two first met. In one narrative, Saul is depressed and one of his servants recommends that he seek a good harpist to cheer him up.

And Saul said unto his servants, Provide me now a man that can play well, and bring him to me. Then answered one of the servants, and said, Behold, I have seen a son of Jesse the Bethlehemite, that is cunning in play-ing. . . . Wherefore Saul sent messengers unto Jesse, and said, Send me David thy son, which is with the sheep. . . . And David came to Saul, and stood before him: and he loved him greatly; and he became his armor-bearer. . . . And it came to pass, when the evil spirit from God was upon Saul, that David took a harp, and played with his hand; so Saul was re-freshed, and was well, and the evil spirit departed from him (1 Sam. 16:17–18, 21, 23).

In a second narrative, a rather celebrated one, David slays Goliath with a stone from his slingshot and cuts off Goliath's head with his sword. David then carries the head of his enemy back to Jerusalem.

> *And David took the head of the Philistine, and brought it to Jerusalem;*
> *but he put his armor in his tent. And when Saul saw David go forth against*
> *the Philistine, he said unto Abner, the captain of the host, Abner, whose son*
> *is this youth? And Abner said, As thy soul liveth, O king, I cannot tell. And*
> *the king said, Inquire thou whose son the stripling is. And as David re-*
> *turned from the slaughter of the Philistine, Abner took him, and brought*
> *him before Saul with the head of the Philistine in his hand. And Saul said*
> *to him, Whose son art thou, thou young man? And David answered, I am*
> *the son of thy servant Jesse the Bethlehemite* (1 Sam. 17:54–58).

Did Saul first meet David when David functioned as a musical therapist? Or did he first meet David after David slew Goliath? These are
two distinct narratives as opposed to the two versions of the death of
Saul.

As for the slaying of Goliath, there appear to be at least three separate versions of this narrative. In the first and no doubt best known of
these, the giant is described as follows:

> *And there went out a champion out of the camp of the Philistines named*
> *Goliath, of Gath, whose height was six cubits and a span. . . . **And the staff***
> ***of his spear was like a weaver's beam*** (1 Sam. 17:4, 7).

It is in this version that David slays Goliath with a slingshot and then
beheads him. In a second version, it is not David but Elhanan who kills
Goliath.

> *And there was again a battle in Gob with the Philistines, where Elhanan*
> *the son of Jaareoregim, a Bethlehemite, slew Goliath the Gittite, **the staff of***
> ***whose spear was like a weaver's beam**. And there was yet a battle in Gath*
> *where was a man of great stature, that had on every hand six fingers, and*
> *on every foot six toes, four and twenty in number; and he also was born to*
> *the giant. And when he defied Israel, Jonathan the son of Shimea the*
> *brother of David slew him* (2 Sam. 19–21).

In the third version, which is close in wording to the second version, it
is Goliath's brother who is killed and also a second giant who is similarly described in terms of polydactylism.

> *And there was war again with the Philistines; and Elhanan the son of*
> *the Jair slew Lahmi the brother of Goliath the Gittite, **whose spear staff***
> ***was like a weaver's beam**. And yet again there was war at Gath, where was*
> *a man of great stature, whose fingers and toes were four and twenty, six on*

each hand, and six on each foot: and he also was the son of the giant. But when he defied Israel, Jonathan the son of Shimea David's brother slew him (1 Chron. 20:5–7).

The repetition of the simile involving a "weaver's beam" supports the idea that these are three different versions of the same incident. It is curious that the very same formula is also found in another episode when one of David's men *"slew an Egyptian, a man of great stature, five cubits high; and in the Egyptian's hand was a spear like a weaver's beam; and he went down to him with a staff, and plucked the spear out of the Egyptian's hand, and slew him with his own spear"* (1 Chron. 11:23). This could possibly be yet a fourth version of the incident insofar as the protagonist uses only a staff, just as David does in the first version: *"And he took his staff in his hand"* (1 Sam. 17:40) and the enemy is depicted as a *"man of great stature,"* a phrase found in the second and third versions. But whether this fourth account is or is not actually a cognate of the other three is not crucial. For it is pretty clear that there are at least three versions of the slaying of Goliath (or his brother).

Regardless of how Saul first came to know David—either as a recommended musical therapist or as the surprising slayer of Goliath—there eventually developed a bitter rivalry between the two. At one point, King Saul seeks to discover where David is hiding. People from Ziph come to Saul and offer to show him David's secret location. In one version, *"Then came up the Ziphites to Saul to Gibeah, saying, Doth not David hide himself with us in strongholds in the wood, in the hill of Hachilah, which is on the south of Jeshimon?"* (1 Sam. 23:19). A second version offers slightly fewer details: *"And the Ziphites came unto Saul to Gibeah, saying, Doth not David hide himself in the hill of Hachilah, which is before Jeshimon?"* (1 Sam. 26:1).

In another legend in which the hunted becomes the hunter, David mercifully spares Saul's life, but he takes a trophy as proof of his deed.

Then Saul took three thousand chosen men out of Israel, and went to seek David and his men upon the rocks of the wild goats. And he came to sheepcotes by the way, where was a cave; and Saul went in to cover his feet: and David and his men remained in the sides of the cave. And the men of David said unto him, Behold the day of which the Lord said unto thee, Behold I will deliver thine enemy into thine hand, that thou mayest do to him as it shall seem good unto thee. **Then David arose, and cut off the skirt of Saul's robe** *privily. And it came to pass afterward, that David's heart smote him, because he had cut off Saul's skirt. And he said unto his men, The*

*Lord forbid that I should do this thing unto my master, the Lord's anointed,
to stretch forth mine hand against him, seeing he is the anointed of the Lord*
(1 Sam. 24:2–6).

The second version of the account includes a report of quite a different
trophy.

> *So David and Abishai came to the people by night; and, behold, Saul lay
> sleeping within the trench, and his spear stuck in the ground at his bolster,
> but Abner and the people lay round about him. Then said Abishai to
> David, God hath delivered thine enemy into thine hand this day: now
> therefore let me smite him, I pray thee, with the spear even to the earth at
> once, and I will not smite him the second time. And David said to Abishai,
> Destroy him not: for who can stretch forth his hand against the Lord's
> anointed, and be guiltless. . . . The Lord forbid that I should stretch forth
> mine hand against the Lord's anointed: but, I pray thee, take thou now the
> spear that is at his bolster and the cruse of water, and let us go.* **So David
> took the spear and the cruse of water from Saul's bolster;** *and they gat
> them away* (1 Sam. 26:7–9, 11–12).

In the first version, it is evidently David himself who cuts off the skirt
of Saul's robe; in the second version, David instructs Abishai to take
Saul's spear and the cruse of water from Saul's bolster. Eventually Saul
is killed, though not by David. As noted earlier, he either dies by his
own hand or is slain by a young Amalekite.

An equally interesting set of versions concerning death is found in
the New Testament. I am thinking of the death of Judas who betrayed
Jesus. In one account, Judas repents. *"And he cast down the pieces of
silver in the temple, and departed, and went and* **hanged himself**" (Matt.
27:5). In a second version, Judas did not return the blood money, and
he died in quite another fashion: *"Now this man purchased a field with
the reward of iniquity; and falling headlong,* **he burst asunder in the
midst and all his bowels gushed out**" (Acts 1:18).

Let us now consider some of the most famous events recounted in
the Bible. One of these events is surely Moses leading his people out of
bondage from Egypt. There appear to be two versions of God ordering
Moses to carry out this important mission. In the first version, God
speaks to Moses from the wondrous "burning bush" at Horeb:

> *And the Angel of the Lord appeared unto him in a flame of fire out of
> the midst of a bush: and he looked and, behold, the bush burned with fire,*

and the bush was not consumed. And Moses said, I will now turn aside, and see this great sight, why the bush is not burnt. And when the Lord saw that he turned aside to see, God called unto him out of the midst of the bush. . . . Moreover he said, I am the God of thy father, the God of Abraham, the God of Isaac, and the God of Jacob. . . . And the Lord said, I have surely seen the affliction of my people which are in Egypt, and have heard their cry by reason of their taskmasters; for I know their sorrows. . . . Come now therefore, and I will send thee unto Pharaoh, that thou mayest bring forth my people the children of Israel out of Egypt (Exod. 3:2–3, 4, 6, 7, 10).

The second version seems to be set in Egypt rather than at Horeb, and there is no mention of a burning bush:

And God spake unto Moses, and said unto him, I am the Lord: And I appeared unto Abraham, unto Isaac, and unto Jacob. . . . And I have also heard the groaning of the children of Israel, whom the Egyptians keep in bondage; and I have remembered my covenant. . . . And the Lord spake unto Moses, saying, Go in, speak unto Pharaoh king of Egypt, that he let the children of Israel go out of his land (Exod. 6:2, 3, 5, 11).

In both versions, Moses seeks to decline the mission on the grounds that he is not a good speaker: "*I am not eloquent, neither heretofore nor since thou has spoken unto thy servant, but I am slow of speech, and of a slow tongue*" (Exod. 4:10). "*How then shall Pharaoh hear me, who am of uncircumcised lips?*" (Exod. 6:12, 30). God insists that Moses do as he is told. Then Moses asks God for a sign that he will be believed. God responds to Moses' request as follows:

And the Lord said unto him, What is that in thine hand? And he said, A rod. And he said, Cast it on the ground. And he cast it on the ground, and it became a serpent (Exod. 4:2–3).

In the second version, Aaron is also involved and in fact, it is Aaron's rod that is transformed into a serpent.

And the Lord spake unto Moses and unto Aaron, saying, When Pharaoh shall speak unto you, saying, Show a miracle for you: then thou shalt say unto Aaron, Take thy rod, and cast it before Pharaoh, and it shall become a serpent (Exodus 7:8–9).

Finally, Moses succeeds in gaining the release of the children of Israel, but when Moses led his people out of Egypt, there was a life-
threatening water shortage. There are two distinct accounts explaining
how Moses obtained water from a rock. In the first, God instructs
Moses to **strike** a rock, a rock upon which God is standing:

> *Behold, I will stand before thee upon the rock in Horeb; and thou shalt*
> **smite** *the rock, and there shall come water out of it, that the people may*
> *drink. And Moses did so in the sight of the elders of Israel* (Exod. 17:6).

In the second version, God tells Moses to **speak** to the rock, and in this
case God does not stand upon it:

> *Take the rod, and gather thou the assembly together, thou and Aaron*
> *thy brother, and* **speak** *ye unto the rock before their eyes; and it shall give*
> *forth his water, and thou shalt bring forth to them water out of the rock: so*
> *thou shalt give the congregation and their beasts drink* (Num. 20:8).

In this second version, however, Moses becomes impatient and "*smote
the rock twice*" (Num. 20:11), and in fact God punishes Moses for dis-
obeying his specific instructions to speak to the rock: "*Because ye believed me not . . . therefore ye shall not bring this congregation into the
land which I have given them*" (Num. 20:12).

There was not only a shortage of water but also a shortage of food.
The children of Israel began to complain, claiming that they had eaten
better back in Egypt (Exod. 16:3; Num. 11:4–5). God hears the com-
plaint and sends a heavy dew followed by a substance called "manna".
There are two versions of the descent of manna from heaven:

> *And it came to pass, that at even the quails came up, and covered the*
> *camp: and in the morning the dew lay round about the host. And when the*
> *dew that lay was gone up, behold, upon the face of the wilderness there lay*
> *a small round thing, as small as the hoar frost on the ground. And when*
> *the children of Israel saw it, they said one to another, It is manna: for they*
> *wist not what it was. And Moses said unto them, This is the bread which*
> *the Lord hath given you to eat. . . . And the house of Israel called the name*
> *thereof Manna: and it was like coriander seed, white; and the taste of it was*
> *like wafers made with honey* (Exod. 16:13–15, 31).

> *And when the dew fell upon the camp in the night, the manna fell upon*
> *it. . . . And the manna was as coriander seed, and the color thereof as the*

color of bdellium. And the people went about, and gathered it, and ground it in mills, or beat it in a mortar, and baked it in pans, and made cakes of it: and the taste of it was as the taste of fresh oil (Num. 11:9, 7–8).

The two versions differ slightly. It is not certain that bdellium is white in color. Honey and fresh oil would not seem to be identical flavors.

Another very well-known dramatic incident in the Old Testament describes the visit of two angels to Lot in the doomed city of Sodom. The angels indicate their intention to spend the night in the street, but Lot insists that they enter his house. They do so and Lot offers them hospitality. Soon, however, a group of Sodomites surround the house and demand that Lot send out the angels to them. Lot responds by offering them his two virgin daughters instead, but to no avail. Here is the relevant portion of that text:

> *And there came two angels to Sodom at even; and Lot sat in the gate of Sodom: and Lot seeing them rose up to meet them. . . . And he said, Behold now, my lords, turn in, I pray you, into your servant's house, and **tarry all night**, and wash your feet, and **ye shall rise up early, and go on your ways.** And they said, Nay; but **we will abide in the street** all night. And he pressed upon them greatly; and they turned in unto him, and entered into his house; and he made them a feast, and did bake unleavened bread, and they did eat. But before they lay down, the men of the city, even the men of Sodom, **compassed the house round**, both old and young, all the people from every quarter: And they called unto Lot, and said unto him, Where are the men which came in to thee this night? **bring them out unto us, that we may know them.** And Lot went out at the door unto them, and shut the door after him, and said, **I pray you, brethren, do not so wickedly.** Behold now, I have **two daughters which have not known man**; let me, I pray you, bring them out unto you, and **do ye to them as is good in your eyes: only unto these men do nothing**; for therefore came they under the shadow of my roof* (Gen. 19:1, 2–8).

This episode is almost certainly familiar to readers, but one that perhaps is not is a narrative in Judges in which an unnamed Levite goes with his servant to Bethlehem to retrieve an unfaithful concubine at her father's house. The concubine's father is very hospitable and repeatedly urges the man to stay longer.

> *And when the man rose up to depart, he, and his concubine, and his servant, his father-in-law, the damsel's father, said unto him, Behold, now the day draweth toward evening, I pray you **tarry all night**: behold, the day*

groweth to an end, lodge here, that thine heart may be merry; and tomor-
*row **get you early on your way,** that thou mayest go home. But the man*
would not tarry that night, but he rose up and departed. . . . And they
passed on and went their way; and the sun went down upon them when
they were by Gibeah. . . . And they turned aside thither, to go in and to
*lodge in Gibeah: and when he went in, he sat him down **in a street** of the*
city: for there was no man that took them into his house to lodging (Judg.
19:9–10, 14, 15).

At this point, an old man (also unnamed) sees the Levite and his concubine and servant in the street and offers them hospitality:

Yet there is both straw and provender for our asses; and there is bread
and wine also for me, and for thy handmaid, and for the young man which
is with thy servants: there is no want of any thing. And the old man said,
Peace be with thee; howsoever, let all thy wants lie upon me; only lodge not
in the street. So he brought him into his house, and gave provender unto
the asses: and they washed their feet, and did eat and drink. Now as they
were making their hearts merry, behold, the men of the city, certain sons of
*Belial, **beset the house round about,** and beat at the door, and spake to the*
*master of the house, the old man, saying, **Bring forth the man that came***
***into thine house, that we may know him.** And the man, the master of the*
house, went out unto them, and said unto them, Nay, my brethren, nay, I
***pray you, do not so wickedly;** seeing that this man is come into mine house,*
*do not this folly. Behold, there **is my daughter a maiden,** and his concu-*
*bine; them I will bring out now, and humble ye them, and **do with them***
what seemeth good unto you, but unto this man do not so vile a thing
(Judg. 19:19–23).

From a folkloristic perspective, there seems little doubt that these are
two versions of the same story. The Sodomites in the first version are
replaced in the second version by the sons of Belial. Belial is an alternative name for Satan or the devil. It contains the kernel "Bel" which is
very likely cognate with the name Baal, the principal male deity of the
Philistines, who from the Judeo-Christian point of view would represent the quintessential false god. We find the same kernel in **Beel**zebub,
the prince of the devils (Matthew 12:24). The parallels in the two
texts—such details as the offering of a virgin daughter to placate the
Sodomites/sons of Belial, plus the striking phraseological similarities—
simply cannot be attributed to polygenetic coincidence. Of course,
there are differences in the two stories, but that is to be expected. It is
what is meant by the "variation" aspect of the folkloristic definitional

criteria of "multiple existence and variation". We can once again demonstrate these criteria in the New Testament.

There are two versions of the so-called Sermon on the Mount. Perhaps the best-known version is reported in Matthew's Gospel:

> *And seeing the multitudes, he went* **up** *into a* **mountain:** *and when he was set, his disciples came unto him: And he opened his mouth, and taught them, saying, Blessed are the poor in spirit: for theirs is the kingdom of heaven. Blessed are they that mourn: for they shall be comforted. Blessed are the meek: for they shall inherit the earth. Blessed are they which do hunger and thirst after righteousness: for they shall be filled. Blessed are the merciful: for they shall obtain mercy. Blessed are the pure in heart: for they shall see God. Blessed are the peacemakers: for they shall be called the children of God. Blessed are they which are persecuted for righteousness' sake: for theirs is the kingdom of heaven. Blessed are ye, when men shall revile you, and persecute you, and shall say all manner of evil against you falsely, for my sake. Rejoice, and be exceeding glad: for great is your reward in heaven: for so persecuted they the prophets which were before you* (Matt. 5:1–12).

Luke's version is much shorter:

> *And he came* **down** *with them and stood in the* **plain.** *. . . . And he lifted up his eyes on his disciples, and said, Blessed be ye poor: for yours is the kingdom of God. Blessed are ye that hunger now: for ye shall be filled. Blessed are ye that weep now: for ye shall laugh. Blessed are ye, when men shall hate you, and when they shall separate you from their company, and shall reproach you, and cast out your name as evil, for the Son of man's sake. Rejoice ye in that day, and leap for joy: for, behold, your reward is great in heaven: for in the like manner did their fathers unto the prophets* (Luke 6:17, 20–23).

This is quite a different sermon. For one thing, Matthew reports that Jesus *"went* **up** *into a* **mountain,"** while Luke indicates that Jesus *"came* **down** *. . . and stood in the* **plain."** If it were decided not to give priority to Matthew's version and rather to respect Luke's version, the Sermon on the Mount might be known instead as the "Sermon in the Plain." The versions of the same sermon also differ with respect to content. "Blessed are the meek" does not appear in Luke's version; Luke's account of "Blessed are ye that weep" does not appear in Matthew's version. Of course, both elements might have been included in the original sermon, but the point is that both elements together do not appear in either Matthew's or Luke's reporting of the sermon. There are also minor variations in wording in the different versions of the same beatitudes. For example, in Luke (6:20) we find *"Blessed be ye poor: for **yours** is the kingdom of **God**"* as opposed to Matthew (5:3): *"Blessed are the poor **in spirit**: for **theirs** is the kingdom of **heaven**."* There is surely a semantic difference between being "poor"—that is, being without material wealth—and being "poor in spirit," that is, being spiritually impoverished. In the light of such variation, we can reasonably conclude that the sermon on the mount or in the plain is a undeniable prima facie example of folklore.

Someone unfamiliar with folklore might assume—wrongly—that fixed-phrase items such as beatitudes or proverbs would not exhibit variation. But fixed-phrase folklore, like all folklore, does indeed manifest multiple existence and variation, as we have seen. Consider Matthew 7:16: *"Ye shall know them by their fruits. Do men gather grapes of thorns, or figs of thistles?"* This is clearly a variant of *"Wherefore by their fruits ye shall know them"* (Matt. 6:20). Compare these with Luke's version: *"For every tree is known by his own fruit. For of thorns men do not gather figs, nor of a bramble bush gather they grapes"* (Luke 6:44). Matthew speaks of gathering **grapes** from thorns; Luke speaks of gathering **figs** from thorns. Matthew speaks of gathering **figs** from thistles; Luke speaks of gathering **grapes** from bramble bushes, the equivalent of thistles.

Proverbs and other fixed-phrase formulas exhibit variation as one would expect of any folkloristic phenomena. An example of this is afforded by the phrase "salt of the earth." It is found in Matthew:

> *Ye are the salt of the earth: but if the salt have lost his savor, wherewith shall it be salted? it is thenceforth good for nothing, but to be cast out, and to be trodden under foot of men* (Matt. 5:13).

Matthew's version comes virtually at the end of the Sermon on the Mount. Mark does not report that sermon, but he does include a version of the phrase:

> *Salt is good: but if the salt have lost his saltiness, wherewith will ye season it? Have salt in yourselves, and have peace one with another* (Mark 9:50).

Luke does give an account of the Sermon (in the Plain), but his version of the phrase occurs elsewhere in his Gospel:

Salt is good: but if the salt have lost his savor, wherewith shall it be seasoned? it is neither fit for the land, nor yet for the dunghill; but men cast it out (Luke 14:34–35).

It is easy to see that these three versions are cognate but also that they are not verbatim identical. Luke's version includes some elements that are found in Mark's, for example, *"Salt is good"* and *"wherewith will ye season it?"* but also some elements that are in Matthew's, for example, *"but if the salt have lost his savor"* and *"to be cast out."* This is a common occurrence in folklore, whereby different versions contain different combinations of elements found in the same basic item. It is also noteworthy that the actual phrase *"salt of the earth"* is found only in Matthew's version.

There are other instances in which a well-known phrase occurs as a variant. Take, for example, the quotation in the transfiguration scene when God speaks as a voice out of a cloud:

*While he [Peter] yet spake, behold, a bright cloud overshadowed them: and behold a voice out of the cloud, which said, This is my beloved Son, **in whom I am well pleased**; hear ye him* (Matt. 17:5; cf. 2 Pet. 1:17).

In other versions of the transfiguration scene, the phrase is absent.

And there was a cloud that overshadowed them: and voice came out of the cloud, saying, This is my beloved Son: hear him (Mark 9:7).

While he thus spake, there came a cloud, and overshadowed them: and they feared as they entered into the cloud. And there came a voice out of the cloud, saying, This is my beloved Son: hear him (Luke 9:34–35).

How then can we be absolutely certain that the phrase "in whom I am well pleased" is in fact traditional? One piece of evidence is that the phrase is reported by Mark, although not in his account of the transfiguration scene. He placed it at a different point in the life of Jesus, namely, directly following the baptism of Jesus by John the Baptist:

*And there came a voice from heaven, saying, Thou art my beloved Son, **in whom I am well pleased*** (Mark 1:11).

Actually, Matthew also used the phrase at the end of his report of Jesus' baptism (3:17). From this we may conclude that the "in whom I am well pleased" formula is certainly traditional even though it occurs in only one of the three Gospel accounts of the transfiguration.

There are still better examples of the variation exhibited by fixed-phrase formulas in the Bible. In Matthew, we have one occurrence of *"He that hath ears to hear, let him hear"* (11:15) and two instances of *"Who hath ears to hear, let him hear"* (13:9 and 13:43). Mark in a single chapter has *"He that hath ears to hear, let him hear"* (4:9) and *"If any man have ears to hear, let him hear"* (4:23). Luke has two examples of *"He that hath ears to hear, let him hear"* (8:8 and 14:35), but in Revelation we find a variant: *"He who has an ear, let him hear what the spirit saith unto the churches"* (2:7, 2:11; 2:17, 3:6, 3:13, 3:22). On the other hand, we also find in Revelation *"If any man have an ear, let him hear"* (13:9), which is close to one of the versions in Mark (4:23). Which of these is the "correct" version? From a folkloristic perspective, there is no such thing as a correct version; there are only versions (plural), all of which are presumably equally traditional and therefore equally correct. It is also worth remarking that the idiom itself in whatever form it may take is per se a confirmation of the oral—as opposed to written—source of biblical wisdom. Consider the opening lines of Psalm 78:

> *Give ear, O my people, to my law: incline your ears to the words of my mouth. I will open my mouth in a parable: I will utter dark sayings of old; Which we have heard and known, and our fathers have told us* (Ps. 78:1–3).

Another obvious and instructive example of a fixed-phrase formula exhibiting variation is the "eat, drink, and be merry" formula. There are five versions in Ecclesiastes alone:

> *There is nothing better for a man than that he should eat and drink, and that he should make his soul enjoy good in his labor. This also I saw, that it was from the hand of God* (Eccles. 2:24).

> *And also that every man should eat and drink, and enjoy the good of all his labor, it is the gift of God* (Eccles. 3:13).

> *Behold that which I have seen: it is good and comely for one to eat and to drink, and to enjoy the good of all his labor that he taketh under the sun all the days of his life, which God giveth him: for it is his portion* (Eccles. 5:18).

Then I commended mirth, because a man hath no better thing under the sun, than to eat, and to drink, and to be merry: for that shall abide with him of his labor the days of his life, which God giveth him under the sun (Eccles. 8:16).

Go thy way, eat thy bread with joy, and drink thy wine with a merry heart: for God now accepteth thy works (Eccles. 9:7).

The "eat, drink, and be merry" exhortation is also found elsewhere in the Bible. There is *"Arise, and eat bread and let thine heart be merry"* (1 Kings 21:7). Perhaps the most familiar rendering is: *"Let us eat and drink; for tomorrow we shall die"* (Isa. 22:13). It is found in the New Testament as well: *"And I will say to my soul, Soul, thou hast much goods laid up for many years; take thine ease, eat, drink, and be merry"* (Luke 12:19). And in the famous parable of the prodigal son, we have the line: *"And bring hither the fatted calf, and kill it; and let us eat and be merry"* (Luke 15:23).

There are far too many proverbs in the Bible to discuss them all, but it is easy enough to sample several of those with clear-cut variation. In one instance, the Bible makes an explicit reference to an item as a proverb, and this is not in the Book of Proverbs.

The word of the Lord came unto me again, saying, What mean ye, that ye use this proverb concerning the land of Israel, saying, The fathers have eaten sour grapes, and the children's teeth are set on edge? As I live, saith the Lord God, ye shall not have occasion any more to use this proverb in Israel (Ezek. 18:1–3).

Not only does God Himself refer to this saying as a proverb, but he promises that the negative situation referred to will never again be found in Israel, thereby ensuring that the future citation of this proverb will not be necessary. Since this is evidently a traditional proverb, we should expect to find other versions of it, and indeed we do:

In those days they shall say no more, The fathers have eaten a sour grape, and the children's teeth are set on edge. But every one shall die for his own iniquity: every man that eateth the sour grape, his teeth shall be set on edge (Jer. 31:29–30).

Although the grape is singular rather than plural, the two passages are clearly cognate, and, furthermore, since God has declared the saying a proverb, we certainly have good reason to accept the saying as such. Evidence for its proverbial status is provided by its inclusion in a modern collection of Lebanese proverbs: "The fathers eat sour grapes and their children's teeth are set on edge" (Frayha 1953:1:201). Of course, this oral version might simply be an echo of the Old Testament tradition, but then again, it might well represent the original oral tradition from which the Old Testament texts were derived. In any case, the meaning of the proverb would clearly appear to be that children pay for the sins of their fathers, that is, the fathers eat something sour, but it is the children's mouths which suffer the consequences.

An interesting instance of proverb variation is illustrated by diverse versions of "A house divided against itself cannot stand" (Mieder 1998). Consider the following three versions:

> *Every kingdom divided against itself is brought* **to desolation** *and* **every city** *or house divided against itself shall not stand* (Matt. 12:25).

> *Every kingdom divided against itself is brought* **to desolation;** *and a house divided against a house falleth* (Luke 11:17).

> *And if a kingdom be divided against itself, that kingdom cannot stand. And if a house be divided against itself, that house cannot stand* (Mark 3:24–25).

Matthew and Luke's versions contain a reference to "desolation," but Mark's does not. Matthew's version refers to "every city," but Luke's and Mark's do not. The variations are minor, but they are variations nonetheless. This again confirms the fact that fixed-phrase items of folklore do manifest variation.

Another excellent example of proverb variation is provided by one of the most celebrated biblical proverbs:

> *A prophet is not without honor, save in his own country, and in his own house* (Matt. 13:57).

> *A prophet is not without honor, but in his own country, and among his own kin, and in his own house* (Mark 6:4).

> *No prophet is accepted in his own country* (Luke 4:24).

For Jesus himself testified, that a prophet hath no honor in his own country (John 4:44).

Sometimes multiple versions of folklore texts seem to produce inconsistencies and contradictions. This can happen with proverbs.

*Answer **not** a fool according to his folly, lest thou also be like unto him* (Prov. 26:4).

Answer a fool according to his folly, lest he be wise in his own conceit (Prov. 26:5).

Perhaps these are really separate proverbs, but they do recommend opposite courses of action. A more apt example might be the following:

Those that seek me early shall find me (Prov. 8:17).

*They shall seek me early, but they shall **not** find me* (Prov. 1:28).

Of course, not all variants of proverbs are contradictory. Consider the following two proverb versions that occur in the same Gospel:

*But many that are **first** shall be **last**; and the **last** shall be **first*** (Matt. 19:30).

*So the **last** shall be **first**, and the **first** last* (Matt. 20:16).

This is an instance of sequential variation. The critical difference has to do with whether "first" comes before "last" or "last" comes before "first," sequentially speaking, in the initial segment of the proverb. We may logically assume that each of the above is a distinct version of the proverb because we have another version of each:

*But many that are **first** shall be **last**; and the **last** first* (Mark 10:31).

*And, behold, there are **last** which shall be **first**; and there are **first** which shall be **last*** (Luke 13:30).

Here is another example of two versions of a proverb in the same Gospel:

For he that is not against us is for us (Luke 9:50).

He that is not with me is against me (Luke 11:23).

Again, we have additional versions of each of these:

> *For he that is not against us is on our part* (Mark 9:40).

> *He that is not with me is against me* (Matt. 12:30).

A handsome example of multiple existence and variation refers to the value and necessity of faith. Even the tiniest bit of faith can bring about miracles. One of the most memorable similes for a tiny bit of faith is the mustard seed. When the disciples ask Jesus why they could not cast out a devil from a sick child, he answers that it is strictly a matter of faith:

> *And Jesus said unto them, Because of your unbelief: for verily I say unto you, If ye have faith as a grain of mustard seed, ye shall say unto this moun-tain, Remove hence to yonder place and it shall remove: and nothing shall be impossible unto you* (Matt. 17:20).

Matthew provides a second version of this image. When the disciples marvel at how quickly a fig tree cursed by Jesus withered away, the fol-lowing response is evoked:

> *Jesus answered and said unto them, Verily I say unto you, If ye have faith, and doubt not, ye shall not only do this which is done to the fig tree, but also if ye shall say unto this mountain, Be thou removed, and be thou cast into the sea; it shall be done. And in all things, whatsoever ye shall ask in prayer, believing, ye shall receive* (Matt. 21:21–22).

This second version is a bit more specific. It is not just that faith can move mountains; it can move them into the sea. Mark's version also comes in response to the fig-withering episode:

> *And Jesus answering saith unto them, Have faith in God. For verily I say unto you, That whosoever shall say unto this mountain, Be thou removed, and be thou cast into the sea; and shall not doubt in his heart, but shall believe that those things which he saith shall come to pass; he shall have whatsoever he saith. Therefore I say unto you, What things soever ye desire, when ye pray, believe that ye receive them, and ye shall have them* (Mark 11:22–24).

The echo of this image in 1 Corinthians refers only to the basic idea of faith moving mountains: *"And though I have all faith, so that I could remove mountains, and have not charity, I am nothing"* (1 Cor. 13:2).

The Gospel of Thomas contains two versions of the image (Cartlidge and Dungan 1994:23, 28), but in both instances it is not faith but evidently peace that moves mountains:

> *Jesus said, "If two make peace between themselves in the same house, they shall say to the mountain, 'Move away,' and it will move"* (Thomas 48).

It is worth remarking that the two versions in Thomas are not verbatim identical by any means.

> *Jesus said, "When you make the two one, you shall be Sons of Man, and when you say, 'Mountain, move away,' it will move"* (Thomas 106).

Finally, Luke's version occurs independently of any mention of a withering fig tree:

> *And the Lord said, If ye had faith as a grain of mustard seed, ye might say unto this sycamine tree, Be thou plucked up by the root, and be thou planted in the sea; and it should obey you* (Luke 17:6).

If we summarize the variation, we have faith (or peace) that can move mountains, faith that can move mountains into the sea, and faith that can move a tree into the sea.

There is another interesting example of two versions of a proverb found in the same Gospel. It is the admonition against hiding one's light under a bushel, a traditional expression still current in popular folk tradition. The first of the two versions in Luke goes as follows:

> *No man when he hath lighted a candle, covereth it with a vessel, or putteth it under a bed; but setteth it on a candlestick, that they which enter in may see the light. For nothing is secret, that shall not be made manifest; neither any thing hid, that shall not be known and come abroad* (Luke 8:16–17).

The second version in Luke does not have the two above elements in the exact same sequence. Rather they are separated by several dozen verses:

> *No man, when he hath lighted a candle, putteth it in a secret place, nei-*
> *ther under a bushel, but on a candlestick, that they which come in may see*
> *the light. . . . For there is nothing covered, that shall not be revealed; neither*
> *hid, that shall not be known* (Luke 11:33, 12:2).

This second version also differs with respect to content, as we have no mention of a vessel or bed but rather a bushel. Now the question might be raised as to whether the two elements belong together in immediate sequence or whether they are separate elements that do not necessarily follow one another. The version in Mark suggests that the two elements do form a coherent unit:

> *And he said unto them, Is a candle brought to be put under a bushel, or*
> *under a bed? and not to be set on a candlestick? For there is nothing hid,*
> *which shall not be manifested, neither was any thing kept secret, but that it*
> *should come abroad* (Mark 4:21–22).

It is noteworthy that in Mark's version we have both a bed and a bushel. In Matthew's version, however, we have only a bushel and no bed. But the two elements are separated by quite a few chapters, which suggests that they may be considered two distinct verses:

> *Neither do men light a candle, and put it under a bushel, but on a can-*
> *dlestick; and it giveth light unto all that are in the house. . . . Fear them not*
> *therefore: for there is nothing covered, that shall not be revealed; and hid,*
> *that shall not be known* (Matt. 5:15, 10:26).

For the record, we should note that the occurrence of two versions of one and the same proverb in Luke is not unique. Consider the following two passages from Luke:

> *For whosoever exalteth himself shall be abased; and he that humbleth*
> *himself shall be exalted* (Luke 14:11).

> *For every one that exalteth himself shall be abased; and he that humbleth*
> *himself shall be exalted* (Luke 18:14).

And it is also found in Matthew:

> *And whosoever shall exalt himself shall be abased; and he that shall*
> *humble himself shall be exalted* (Matt. 23:12).

The occurrence of proverb doublets in the same Gospel is by no means confined to Luke. Here are two passages from Matthew:

> *And he that taketh not his cross, and followeth after me, is not worthy of me. He that findeth his life shall lose it: and he that loseth his life for my sake shall find it* (Matt. 10:38–39).

> *Then said Jesus unto his disciples, If any man will come after me, let him deny himself, and take up his cross, and follow me. For whosoever will save his life shall lose it: and whosoever will lose his life for my sake shall find it* (Matt. 16:24–25).

Mark has only one version of the life-saving/life-losing proverb, but it is combined with the initial plea for the true follower to take up the cross:

> *And when he had called the people unto him with his disciples also, he said unto them, Whosoever will come after me, let him deny himself, and take up his cross, and follow me. For whosoever will save his life shall lose it: but whosoever shall lose his life for my sake and the gospel's, the same shall save it* (Mark 8:34–35).

On the basis of these three versions, one might well assume that the two elements are part of a coherent, logical unit, that is, that the reference to the cross invariably precedes the life-saving proverb. We find a version in Luke that supports this premise:

> *And he said to them all, If any man will come after me, let him deny himself, and take up his cross daily, and follow me. For whosoever will save his life shall lose it: but whosoever will lose his life for my sake, the same shall save it* (Luke 9:23–24).

On the other hand, we find a second version of the proverb in Luke in which the two elements are separated by several chapters:

> *And whosoever doth not bear his cross, and come after me, cannot be my disciple. . . . Whosoever shall seek to save his life shall lose it; and whosoever shall lose his life shall preserve it* (Luke 14:27, 17:33).

The case for the independence of the life-saving proverb is supported by its occurrence in John (with variation in wording) without any tie to a "cross" preamble. It is, however, **followed** by a line that is reminiscent of the preamble, despite the lack of reference to the cross. If it is a form of the preamble, then we would have a case of sequence variation:

> *He that loveth his life shall lose it; and he that hateth his life in this world shall keep it unto life eternal. If any man serve me, let him follow me* (John 12:25–26).

The way in which individual verses can sometimes appear in isolation and at other times in combination with other verses is surely reminiscent of oral tradition. In folk songs, there may be a floating stanza that occurs in quite diverse song texts, and the same holds for individual narrative motifs. Even folktales may reflect the same tendency. For example, Aarne-Thompson tale type 480, The Tale of the Kind and the Unkind Girls (in which a kind girl treats a donor figure well and is rewarded by being showered with gold or having gold, pearls, or flowers fall from her mouth, but an unkind girl who is rude to the same donor figure is subsequently punished by being showered with pitch or having frogs or toads leap from her mouth) does occur as an independent folktale, but it can also be found as an introduction to Aarne-Thompson tale type 510A, Cinderella (cf. Roberts 1994:102, 113–4).

There are many instances of this in the Bible. For example, Psalm 108 has only thirteen elements. The first five elements are the same as the last five elements in Psalm 57, that is, Psalm 108:1–5 = Psalm 57:6–11, while the last eight elements are the same as the last eight elements of Psalm 60, that is, Psalm 108:6–13 = Psalm 60:5–12.

In the same way, we can easily demonstrate that a passage in Jeremiah consists of a patchwork of several passages from Isaiah:

Jeremiah	Isaiah
We have heard the pride of Moab, (he is exceeding proud), his loftiness, and his arrogancy, and his pride, and the haughtiness of his heart. I know his wrath, saith the Lord; but it shall not be so; his lies shall not so effect it (48:29–30).	*We have heard of the pride of Moab; he is very proud: even of his haughtiness, and his pride, and his wrath: but his lies shall not be so (16:6).*
From the cry of Heshbon even unto Elealeh, and even unto Jahaz, have they uttered their voice, from Zoar	*And Heshbon shall cry, and Elealeh: their voice shall be heard even unto Jahaz. . . . My heart shall cry out for*

even unto Horonaim, as a heifer of three years old; for the waters also of Nimrim shall be desolate (48:34).	*Moab; his fugitives shall flee unto Zoar, a heifer of three years old . . . for in the way of Horonaim they shall raise up a cry of destruction. For the waters of Nimrim shall be desolate (15:4–6).*
For every head shall be bald, and every beard clipped: upon all the hands shall be cuttings, and upon the loins sackcloth (48:37).	*On all their heads shall be baldness, and every beard cut off. In their streets they shall gird themselves with sackcloth (15:2–3).*

What occurs more or less in sequence in Jeremiah 48 is found in a different order in Isaiah. In this illustration, the Jeremiah sequence appears to be made up of three pieces of Isaiah, namely, Isaiah 16:6, 15:4–6, and 15:2–3. Two different chapters of Isaiah are involved, and the two sections of chapter 15 are found in reverse order in Jeremiah. If one wanted to assume that Isaiah was the primary source, then it would be a matter of Jeremiah's version having altered the sequence. I am not so much interested in seeking to ascertain the relative priority of the parallels, but rather to demonstrate that the Jeremiah version contains a combination of elements from Isaiah, another clue that we are dealing with a derivative of oral tradition. Of course, literary texts can also be composed by combining earlier written sources in new ways, but this combinatorial feature is certainly consistent with a hypothesis that the Bible is codified oral tradition.

Another striking example of how one passage in the Bible may be shown to be composed of virtually identical portions of other passages occurs in 1 Chronicles 16, in which King David, to celebrate the recovery of the ark of the covenant, composed a psalm. However, the initial dozen or so lines of this psalm are basically the same as those found in Psalm 105. In other words, 1 Chronicles 16:8–23 is essentially Psalm 105:1–15. Moreover, the next lines, namely, 1 Chronicles 16:23–33, constitute a version of all thirteen lines of Psalm 96. But 1 Chronicles 16 is not just a combination of the initial segment of Psalm 105 and the totality of Psalm 96. The next two lines of 1 Chronicles 16 are parallel to lines in Psalm 107 and 106:

O give thanks unto the Lord; for he is good; for his mercy endureth forever. And say ye, Save us, O God of salvation, and gather us together, and deliver us from the heathen, that we may give thanks to thy holy name, and glory in thy praise (1 Chron. 16:34–35).

O Give thanks unto the Lord, for he is good: for his mercy endureth for ever (Ps. 107:1). *Save us, O Lord our God, and gather us from among the heathen, to give thanks unto thy holy name, and to triumph in thy praise* (Ps. 106:47).

Folklorists know well that in folk songs one often finds stanzas that seem to move freely from one song to another. Here in the psalm cited in 1 Chronicles 16 we find elements from at least four different psalms. Is this unusual? Not at all if it's folklore. It is the norm rather than the exception.

But let us return to the proverb genre once again. It is really quite fascinating to observe the degrees of variation in fixed-phrase genres such as proverbs. There is one describing how a maleficent digger of a pit may himself fall into it.

Whosoever causeth the righteous to go astray in an evil way, he shall fall himself into his own pit (Prov. 28:10).

This seems to be the same proverb as one found in the Psalms:

He made a pit, and digged it, and is fallen into the ditch which he made (Ps. 7:15).

Here is a third version, also from the Book of Proverbs:

Whoso diggeth a pit shall fall therein: and he that rolleth a stone, it will return upon him (Prov. 26:27).

This third version is expanded to include a stone-rolling image, an image found in a fourth version that is even more comprehensive:

He that diggeth a pit shall fall into it; and whoso breaketh a hedge, a serpent shall bite him. Whoso removeth stones shall be hurt therewith; and he that cleaveth wood shall be endangered thereby (Eccles. 10:8–9).

No folklorist would have the slightest doubt that these represent four versions of the same proverb. They are cognate, but not identical. In some cases in the Bible, however, the duplicate passages are such that the texts are almost identical. An illustration of this is the celebrated metaphorical articulation of a wish for peace in which swords are beaten into plowshares. An issue arising from these duplicate texts, however, is, Who uttered this well-wrought wish? Was it Isaiah or was it Micah?

The book of the prophet Isaiah begins as follows:

> *The vision of Isaiah the son of Amoz which he saw concerning Judah and Jerusalem in the days of Uzziah, Jotham, Ahaz, and Hezekiah, kings of Judah. Hear, O heavens, and give ear, O earth* (Isa. 1:1–2).

The book of Micah begins as follows:

> *The word of the Lord that came to Micah the Morasthite in the days of Jotham, Ahaz, and Hezekiah, kings of Judah, which he saw concerning Samaria and Jerusalem. Hear, all ye people: hearken, O earth* (Mic. 1:1–2).

In theory, these two similar beginnings might be thought to be mere coincidental parallels, attributable to stylistic features of opening statements. But if one compares Isaiah 2:2–4 with Micah 4:1–3, one finds virtually identical passages. We shall illustrate this by comparing the portion of the duplicate texts that include the swords-into-plowshares metaphor.

Isaiah 2:4	*Micah 4:3*
And he shall judge among the nations, and shall rebuke many people: and they shall beat their swords into plowshares, and their spears pruning hooks; nation shall not lift up sword against nation, neither shall they learn war any more.	*And he shall judge among many people, and rebuke strong nations afar off; and they shall beat their swords into plowshares, and their spears into pruning hooks: nation shall not lift up a sword against nation, neither shall they learn war any more.*

So who should be given credit for this memorable metaphor—Isaiah or Micah? The metaphor is very likely a traditional one, coming from oral tradition. Evidence comes from Joel. First we should remark that Joel is specifically instructed by God to pass on *"the word of the Lord"* via oral tradition. The divine injunction occurs at the very beginning of the book of Joel:

Tell ye your children of it, and let your children tell their children, and their children another generation (Joel 1:3).

This injunction, incidentally, is a pointed reminder that it was understood that the Bible was supposed to be transmitted **orally** from generation to generation. In any case, later God employs the plowshares metaphor although in reverse:

Beat your plowshares into swords, and your pruning hooks into spears: let the weak say, I am strong (Joel 23:10).

Once again, we have multiple existence and variation, the unmistakable signs of authentic oral tradition, that is, folklore.

The question of whether Isaiah or Micah should be credited with the sword-plowshare metaphor is a type of question very familiar to folklorists, who often find that floating or migratory legends, for example, frequently become attached to a variety of different historical figures. It is not always possible to determine which of these figures was the first to participate in the legend under consideration. The point is that it is common to find the identical legendary account told about two or more totally distinct personages. There are numerous illustrations of this in the Bible. One of these has to do with an alleged rumor related by God Himself. The issue revolves around whether this rumor was communicated to Obadiah or to Jeremiah. In this context, it may be instructive to compare the first portion of the book of Obadiah with the relevant passages in Jeremiah:

The vision of Obadiah. Thus saith the Lord God concerning Edom; We have heard a rumor from the Lord, and an ambassador is sent among the heathen, Arise ye, and let us rise up against her in battle. Behold, I have made thee small among the heathen: thou are greatly despised. . . . Though thou exalt thyself as the eagle, and though thou set thy nest among the stars, thence will I bring thee down, saith the Lord. If thieves came to thee, if robbers by night, (how art thou cut off!) would they not have stolen till they had enough? if the grape gatherers came to thee, would they not leave some grapes? How are the things of Esau searched out! how are his hidden things sought up! (Obad. 1–6).

I have heard a rumor from the Lord, and an ambassador is sent unto the heathen, saying, Gather ye together, and come against her, and rise up to the battle. For, lo, I will make thee small among the heathen, and despised among men. Thy terribleness hath deceived thee, and the pride of thine heart, O thou that dwellest in the clefts of the rock, that holdest the height of the hill: though thou shouldest make thy nest as high as the eagle, I will bring thee down from thence, saith the Lord (Jer. 49:14–16). *If grape gatherers come to thee, would they not leave some grapes? if thieves by night, they will destroy till they have enough. But I have made Esau bare, I have uncovered his secret places, and he shall not be able to hide himself . . .* (Jer. 49:9–10).

There can be absolutely no doubt that these are two versions of the same incident. They are certainly cognate, but there is some interesting variation. The issue of whether credit for reporting the rumor belongs to Jeremiah or to Obadiah is perhaps moot. It is nonetheless a prime example of multiple existence and variation in the Bible.

I cannot help wondering how many ordinary readers of the Bible (as opposed to Bible scholars) are fully aware of the large number of duplicate or repeated passages it contains. And if they are aware of them, do they realize the implications of such repetitions? Let me give several additional examples.

An extensive doublet occurs in the case of 2 Kings 18:13, 17–37 and Isaiah 36:1–22. A modern editor would surely have noticed, for example, that the doublet continues inasmuch as 2 Kings 19 and Isaiah 37 are nearly identical. There is no need to cite both passages in extenso. A single passage should suffice:

> *But Rab-sha-keh said **unto them,** hath my master sent me to thy master and to thee, to speak these words? hath he not sent me to the men which sit on the wall, that they may eat their own dung, and drink their own piss with you?* (2 Kings 18:27).

> *But Rab sha-keh said, Hath my master sent me to thy master and to thee to speak these words? hath he not sent me to the men that sit upon the wall that they may eat their own dung, and drink their own piss with you?* (Isa. 36:12).

The first passage includes "unto them," but otherwise the two passages are almost identical. It cannot be stressed enough that such duplication in the Bible is by no means an isolated occurrence. There are many such duplicate passages that, presumably because of their hallowed status, were not eliminated by devout scribes and editors.

Another extended set of duplicate passages consists of 1 Kings

22:4–35 and 2 Chronicles 18:3–34. Again, it is almost certain that a modern secular copy editor would have deleted one of these two nearly identical passages. It should be sufficient to compare just the beginnings of the two sequences involving a conversation between Ahab, the king of Israel, and Jehoshaphat, the king of Judah:

> *And he said unto Jehoshaphat, Wilt thou go with me to battle to Ramothgilead? And Jehoshaphat said to the king of Israel, I am as thou art, my people as thy people, my horses as thy horses* (1 Kings 22:4).

> *And Ahab king of Israel said unto Jehoshaphat king of Judah, Wilt thou go with me to Ramothgilead? And he answered him, I am as thou art, and my people as thy people; and we will be with thee in the war* (2 Chron. 18:3).

Another striking set of duplicate texts consists of accounts of David's moving the ark from one location to another in 2 Samuel 6:12–19 and 1 Chronicles 15:26–16:3. A short sample from the two reveals both the cognation of the texts as well as the inevitably fascinating variation:

> *And it was so, that when they that bare the ark of the Lord had gone six paces, he sacrificed oxen and fatlings. And David danced before the Lord with all his might; and David was girded with a linen ephod. So David and all the house of Israel brought up the ark of the Lord with shouting, and with the sound of the trumpet. And as the ark of the Lord came into the city of David, Michal Saul's daughter looked through a window and saw king David leaping and dancing before the Lord; and she despised him in her heart* (2 Sam. 6:13–16).

> *And it came to pass, when God helped the Levites that bare the ark of the covenant of the Lord, that they offered seven bullocks and seven rams. And David was clothed with a robe of fine linen, and all the Levites that bare the ark, and the singers, and Chenaniah the master of the song with the singers: David also had upon him an ephod of linen. Thus all Israel brought up the ark of the covenant of the Lord with shouting, and with the sound of the cornet, and with trumpets, and with cymbals, making a noise with psalteries and harps. And it came to pass, as the ark of the covenant of the Lord came to the city of David, that Michal the daughter of Saul looking out at a window saw king David dancing and playing: and she despised him in her heart* (1 Chron. 125:26–29).

Sometimes the duplicate passages are found in the same book or Gospel. One such instance occurs in Jeremiah. A comparison of Jeremiah 6:12–15 with Jeremiah 8:10–12 easily shows this. Some variation, however, can be observed in the opening pericopes:

> *And their houses shall be turned unto others, with their fields and wives together: for I will stretch out my hand upon the inhabitants of the land, saith the Lord. For from the least of them even unto the greatest of them every one is given to covetousness; and from the prophet even unto the priest every one dealeth falsely* (Jer. 6:12–13).

> *Therefore will I give their wives unto others, and their fields to them that shall inherit them; for every one from the least even unto the greatest is given to covetousness, from the prophet even unto the priest every one dealeth falsely* (Jer. 8:10).

In modern times, a meticulous copy editor or nit-picking proofreader would surely have caught these duplicate passages and requested the author to eliminate one of them. There are other examples in Jeremiah of repeated passages. For example, Jeremiah 50:40–43 combines Jeremiah 49:18 and Jeremiah 6:22–24, and Jeremiah 50:44–46 is parallel to Jeremiah 49:19–21. Jeremiah, it seems, is particularly replete with duplicate passages. Any reader who doubts this should compare Jeremiah 10:12–16 with Jeremiah 51:15–19. The passages are word-for-word identical.

Duplicate passages also occur in the same chapter or book in the New Testament:

> *Then certain of the scribes and of the Pharisees answered, saying Master, we would see a sign from thee. But he answered and said unto them: An evil and adulterous generation seeketh after a sign; and there shall be no sign given to it, but the sign of the prophet Jonas* (Matt. 12:38–39).

> *The Pharisees also with the Sadducees came, and tempting desired him that he would show them a sign from heaven. . . . A wicked and adulterous generation seeketh after a sign; and there shall no sign be given to it, but the sign of the prophet Jonas* (Matt. 16:1, 4).

In this instance there is, besides the two versions in Matthew, a version in Luke:

> *And others, tempting him, sought of him a sign from heaven. . . . And when the people were gathered thick together, he began to say, This is an*

evil generation: they seek a sign; but there shall no sign be given it, but the
sign of Jonas the prophet (Luke 11:16, 29).

In cases where the repetitions occur in the same chapter, they are all the more extraordinary. A typical example is found in chapter 36 of Genesis. Genesis 36:9–14 is essentially repeated immediately as 36:15–18. It is one thing in folklore to repeat a folk song or a joke; it is another to repeat that folk song or joke right after singing or telling it for the first time. Actually, in chapter 36 of Genesis, there are individual passages repeated not just twice but thrice:

> *And Aholibamah bare Jeush, and Jaalam, and Korah: these are the sons of Esau, which were born unto him in the land of Canaan* (Gen. 36:5).

> *And these were the sons of Aholibamah, the daughter of Anah the daughter of Zebeon, Esau's wife: and she bare to Esau Jeush, and Jaalam, and Korah* (Gen. 36:14).

> *And these are the sons of Aholibamah Esau's wife: duke Jeush, duke Jaalam, duke Korah: these were the dukes that came of Aholibamah the daughter of Anah, Esau's wife* (Gen. 36:18).

Here we have threefold repetition and with some variation, a sure sign that we are dealing with oral tradition.

Speaking of Aholibamah, we may comment on the fact that she was only one of Esau's several wives. In one listing of Esau's wives, we learn that Esau disobeyed his father Isaac's instruction not to take "*a wife of the daughters of Canaan*" (Gen. 28:1). Actually the instruction was initially given to Esau's brother Jacob. Isaac's wishes notwithstanding,

> *Esau took his wives of the daughters of Canaan: Adah the daughter of Elon the Hittite, and Aholibamah the daughter of Anah the daughter of Zibeon the Hivite* (Gen. 36:2).

But in another passage we are told:

> *And Esau was forty years old when he took to wife Judith the daughter of Beeri the Hittite, and Bashemath the daughter of Elon the Hittite: Which were a grief of mind unto Isaac and to Rebekah* (Gen. 26:34).

The first passage indicates that Esau married Adah, the daughter of Elon the Hittite, whereas the second reports that he married Bashemath, the daughter of Elon the Hittite. Of course, it was certainly possible in those times to marry two daughters of the same man. But there is yet another version to consider:

> *And Esau seeing that the daughters of Canaan pleased not Isaac his father: Then went Esau unto Ishmael, and took unto the wives which he had Mahalath the daughter of Ishmael, Abraham's son, the sister of Nebajoth, to be his wife* (Gen. 28:8–9).

There is one last passage that is relevant to this matter. Following the first of these passages in which Aholibamah is mentioned, we learn that Esau also married *"Bashemath Ishmael's daughter, sister of Nebajoth"* (Gen. 36:3). The reader who has been able to follow all this may realize that if Esau did marry Bashemath, it is not entirely clear whether Bashemath is the daughter of Elon the Hittite (Gen. 26:34) or of Ishmael (Gen. 36:3). And if Esau did marry a daughter of Ishmael, was her name Mahalath (Gen. 28:9) or Bashemath (Gen. 36:3)?

We find another instance of duplicate passages within a single chapter in chapter 12 of Deuteronomy:

> *Notwithstanding, thou mayest kill and eat flesh in all thy gates, whatsoever thy soul lusteth after, according to the blessing of the Lord thy God which he hath given thee: the unclean and the clean may eat thereof, as of the roebuck and as of the hart. Only ye shall not eat the blood; ye shall pour it upon the earth as water* (Deut. 12:15–16).

> *And thou shalt eat in thy gates whatsoever thy soul lusteth after. Even as the roebuck and the hart is eaten, so thou shalt eat them: the unclean and the clean shall eat of them alike. Only be sure that thou eat not the blood: for the blood is the life; and thou mayest not eat the life with the flesh. Thou shalt not eat it; thou shalt pour it upon the earth as water* (Deut. 12:21–24).

There are parallel passages throughout the Bible. Some occur in just one chapter of one book, some just in one book, some just in the Old Testament, and some in both the Old and New Testaments. Of course, it could be argued that compilers of the New Testament made a conscious effort to refer to or echo passages in the Old Testament and that this could account for parallels. If one examines such parallels, however, one often finds that the Old and New Testament parallels are not verbatim identical, and this would tend to support the idea of oral tradition as a likely source for both the Old and New Testaments. For example, consider the following two passages from the Old and New Testaments, respectively:

> *If thine enemy be hungry, give him bread to eat; and if he be thirsty, give him water to drink: For thou shalt heap coals of fire upon his head, and the Lord shall reward thee* (Prov. 25:21–22).

> *Therefore if thine enemy hunger, feed him; if he thirst, give him drink: for in so doing thou shalt heap coals of fire on his head* (Rom. 12:20).

I mentioned this passage earlier in connection with the legend involving white women in an elevator frightened by an African American man. But the concern here is to show that these two passages are unquestionably cognate, although they are not verbatim identical. The specific mention of bread and water in the Proverbs version is not found in the Romans version.

One can imagine a skeptic conceding that there are indeed multiple versions of some selected passages in both the Old and New Testaments, and further that these duplicate texts are not exactly identical. But what about the most fundamental and basic passages in the Bible? Aren't they more or less stable and consistent? What about the Ten Commandments, for example? What about the Lord's Prayer?

The Ten Commandments

Let us consider the different versions of the Ten Commandments. In Exodus 20, we have the first and probably best-known version:

> *And God spake all these words, saying, I am the Lord thy God, which have brought thee out of the land of Egypt, out of the house of bondage. Thou shalt have no other gods before me. Thou shalt not make unto thee any graven image, or any likeness of any thing that is in heaven above, or that is in the earth below, or that is in the water under the earth: Thou shalt not bow down thyself to them, nor serve them: for I the Lord thy God am a jealous God, visiting the iniquity of the fathers upon the children unto the third and fourth generation of them that hate me. . . . Thou shalt not take the name of the Lord thy God in vain. . . . Remember the sabbath day, to keep it holy. Six days shalt thou labor, and do all thy work: But the sev-*

*enth day is the sabbath of the Lord thy God: in it thou shalt not do any
work. . . . Honor thy father and thy mother. . . . Thou shalt not kill. Thou
shalt not commit adultery. Thou shalt not steal. Thou shalt not bear false
witness against thy neighbor. Thou shalt not covet thy neighbor's house,
thou shalt not covet thy neighbor's wife, nor his manservant, nor his maidservant, nor his ox, nor his ass, nor any thing that is thy neighbor's* (Exod.
20:1–17).

We find a rather abbreviated second version later in Exodus:

*For thou shalt worship no other gods: for the Lord, whose name is Jeal-
ous, is a jealous God* (Exod. 34:14).

*. . . visiting the iniquity of the fathers upon the children, and upon the
children's children, unto the third and to the fourth generation* (Exod.
34:7).

Thou shalt make thee no molten gods (Exod. 34:17).

Six days thou shalt work, but on the seventh day thou shalt rest (Exod.
34:21).

We find another partial version in Leviticus 19. Here are some of the
highlights:

*And the Lord spake unto Moses saying . . . Ye shall fear every man his
mother, and his father, and keep my sabbaths: I am the Lord your God.
Turn ye not unto idols, nor make to yourselves molten gods: I am the Lord
your God. . . . You shall not steal, neither deal falsely, neither lie one to
another, And ye shall not swear by my name falsely, neither shalt thou pro-
fane the name of thy God: I am the Lord. Thou shalt not defraud thy neighbor* (Lev. 19:1, 3–4, 11–13).

Another version of the Ten Commandments is found in Deuteronomy
5. It is quite complete:

*I am the Lord thy God, which brought thee out of the land of Egypt, from
the house of bondage. Thou shalt have none other gods before me. Thou
shalt not make thee any graven image, nor any likeness of any thing that is
in heaven above, nor that is in the earth beneath, or that is in the waters
beneath the earth: thou shalt not bow down thyself unto them, nor serve
them: for I the Lord thy God am a jealous God, visiting the iniquity of the*

fathers upon the children unto the third and fourth generation of them that hate me . . . and keep my commandments. Thou shalt not take the name of the Lord thy God in vain: for the Lord will not hold him guiltless that taketh his name in vain. Keep the sabbath day to sanctify it, as the Lord thy God hath commanded thee. . . . Honor thy father and thy mother. . . . Thou shalt not kill. Neither shalt thou commit adultery. Neither shalt thou steal. Neither shalt thou bear false witness against thy neighbor. Neither shalt thou desire thy neighbor's wife, neither shalt thou covet thy neighbor's house, his field, or his manservant, or his maidservant, his ox, or his ass, or any thing that is thy neighbor's (Deut. 5:6–12, 16–21).

The Deuteronomy version is quite similar to the Exodus version, but considering that the Ten Commandments were supposed to have been written in stone, one would not expect even the slightest variation. Yet in the Exodus version, coveting thy neighbor's house comes **before** coveting thy neighbor's wife, whereas the order is reversed in the Deuteronomy version (Exodus 20:17; Deuteronomy 5:21). This is admittedly only a minor sequential variation, but variation it is.

Perhaps a more provocative question concerning the Ten Commandments is whether there are really ten of them. Although there is a specific mention of the words upon the tables being "the ten commandments" (Exod. 34:28, Deut. 4:13), if one counts the "shalt nots" and "shalt not" equivalents in the Exodus 20 version, one is hard-pressed to identify just ten:

1. *Thou shalt have no other gods before me.*
2. *Thou shalt not make unto thee any graven image.*
3. *Thou shalt not bow down thyself to them, nor serve them.*
4. *Thou shalt not take the name of the Lord thy God in vain.*
5. *Remember the sabbath day, to keep it holy.*
6. *Honor thy father and thy mother.*
7. *Thou shalt not kill.*
8. *Thou shalt not commit adultery.*
9. *Thou shalt not steal.*
10. *Thou shalt not bear false witness against thy neighbor.*
11. *Thou shalt not covet thy neighbor's house.*

These eleven commandments do not include the initial words: *"I am the Lord thy God."* If this were counted as a commandment, that would bring the total to twelve. As it is not in the form of an injunction, there is some resistance to considering this a bona fide commandment. On the other hand, when Jesus was asked, "Which is the first command-ment of all?" his answer was: *"The first of all the commandments is . . . The Lord our God is one Lord"* (Mark 12:28–29). This would tend to suggest that it was indeed considered a "commandment" inasmuch as that was the label Jesus himself allegedly used to refer to the words in question.

There is considerably more variation in the different versions of per-haps the most famous Mosaic law, namely, the so-called *lex talionis:*

> *And if any mischief follow, then thou shalt give life for life, Eye for eye, tooth for tooth, hand for hand, foot for foot, Burning for burning, wound for wound, stripe for stripe* (Exod. 21:23–25).

> *And he that killeth any man shall surely be put to death. And he that killeth a beast shall make it good; beast for beast. And if a man cause a blemish in his neighbor; as he hath done, so shall it be done to him; Breach for breach, eye for eye, tooth for tooth: as he hath caused a blemish in a man, so shall it be done to him again* (Lev. 24:17–20).

> *And thine eye shall not pity; but life shall go for life, eye for eye, tooth for tooth, hand for hand, foot for foot* (Deut. 19:21).

These are three versions of the same traditional law, but the wording varies. It is not certain which of these versions Matthew sought to re-pudiate in the passage: *"Ye have heard that it hath been said, An eye for an eye, and a tooth for a tooth: But I say unto you, That ye resist not evil: but whosoever shall smite thee on thy right cheek, turn to him the other also"* (Matt. 5:38–39). Since the wording as quoted by Matthew does not correspond exactly to any of the three versions in the Old Testa-ment, he may not in fact have meant to refer to any one of them. Moreover, it should be noted that Matthew says, *"Ye have **heard** that it hath been **said**."* Matthew did **not** say, "Ye have **seen** that it hath been **written**." It is likely that Matthew was referring to an oral tradition. This would constitute evidence that this law was part of folk law, that is, part of folklore. Of course, the existence of three distinct versions in the Old Testament is sufficient to demonstrate the item's authenticity as folklore, even without Matthew's allusion to an oral tradition.

Not only is there variation in the different versions of the Ten Com-mandments, albeit slight, but there is even more striking variation in their very transmission or recording. Did God communicate them orally or in writing? Were they first written down by Moses or by God Himself?

Most of our information comes from Exodus. According to Exodus 20:1, *"And God spake all these words saying . . ."* This would strongly suggest that God presented the Commandments initially in oral form. This is confirmed by Exodus 20:22 with such words as *"And the Lord said unto Moses, Thus thou shalt say unto the children of Israel, Ye have seen that I have talked with you from heaven."* This followed the initial proclamation of the Ten Commandments.

This leaves us with the question of how the Ten Commandments came to be written down. According to Exodus 24:4, *"And Moses wrote all the words of the Lord,"* but in the same chapter in Exodus 24:12 we are told, *"And the Lord said unto Moses, Come to me into the mount, and be there: and I will give thee tablets of stone, and a law, and commandments which I have written; that thou mayest teach them."* This states in no uncertain terms that it was God Himself who wrote the Ten Commandments. Another chapter of Exodus corroborates this: *"And he gave unto Moses, when he had made an end of communing with him upon mount Sinai, two tables of testimony, tables of stone, written with the finger of God"* (Exod. 31:18). In another passage, seemingly addressed to Moses, God's authorship is again attested: *"And the Lord spake unto you out of the midst of the fire. . . . And he declared unto you his covenant, which he commanded you to perform, even ten commandments; and he wrote them upon two tables of stone"* (Deut. 4:12, 13).

When Moses returns from his encounter with God to bring the Commandments to the people, there is yet another affirmation of God's role in their recording. *"And Moses turned, and went down from the mount, and the two tables of the testimony were in his hand: the tables were written on both their sides: on the one side and on the other were they written. And the tables were the work of God, and the writing was the writing of God, graven upon the tables"* (Exod. 32:15–16). Moses, however, became so angry about the construction of the golden calf in his absence that he destroyed the first set of tablets. *"And it came to pass, as soon as he came nigh unto the camp, that he saw the calf, and the dancing: and Moses' anger waxed hot, and he cast the tables out of his hands, and brake them beneath the mount"* (Exod. 32:19).

This meant that God had to write down the Commandments again on a second set of tablets.

> *And the Lord said unto Moses: Hew thee two tables of stone like unto the first: and I will write upon these tables the words that were in the first tables, which thou brakest* (Exod. 34:1).

So, once again, we are told that God was the scribe, serving as His own amanuensis. In another version of this event, told in the first person by Moses, we find a similar account:

> *At that time the Lord said unto me, Hew thee two tables of stone like unto the first, and come up unto me into the mount, and make thee an ark of wood. **And I will write on the tables the words that were in the first tables which thou brakest, and thou shalt put them in the ark.** . . . And he wrote on the tables, according to the first writing, the ten commandments* (Deut. 10:1–2).

There are so many statements attesting that God wrote down the Ten Commandments Himself that we might be tempted to dismiss the words in Exodus 24:43: *"And Moses wrote all the words of the Lord"* as an unfortunate error. The problem is that we have yet another explicit version of the event, and in this version God specifically orders Moses to do the writing! *"**And the Lord said unto Moses, Write thou these words:** for after the tenor of these words I have made a covenant with thee and with Israel. And he was there with the Lord forty days and forty nights; he did neither eat bread, nor drink water. And **he wrote upon the tables the words of the covenant, the ten commandments**"* (Exodus 34:27–28). In this version, not only is Moses described as writing down the Ten Commandments, but he does so at the express command of God. From these diverse versions, we can conclude that either God Himself or Moses at God's request wrote down the Ten Commandments. What may be something of a problem for historians or theologians is not a problem for folklorists. Here we have another fine example of multiple existence and variation, the hallmarks of authentic folklore.

There are also different versions of just where and how Moses received the Ten Commandments. According to the version in Exodus, Moses came to God on the top of Mount Sinai (Exodus 19:11, 20), and the people were ordered to keep away. Only Aaron was permitted to accompany him (Exodus 19:24). This is why Moses *"went down unto the people, and spake unto them"* (Exod. 19:25) so as to relay God's commandments to them. But in Deuteronomy, God is said to have proclaimed the Ten Commandments *"in Horeb"* (4:10, 15), not on Mount Sinai, and, furthermore, God instructed Moses, *"Gather me the people together, and I will make them hear my words"* (Deut. 4:10), suggesting that the people could hear God's words for themselves.

One of the other issues arising from the study of the Ten Commandments concerns the nature of the **first** Commandment. The initial
statement in the versions in both Exodus 20 and Deuteronomy 5 is *"I
am the Lord thy God,"* but that is not really in the rhetorical form of
the majority of the Commandments, which begin with "Thou shalt not
. . ." For this reason, the first Commandment is usually said to be
"Thou shalt have no other gods before me."

The relevance of this issue becomes clear when we consider the
Shema, which is the most basic prayer among Jews. At the risk of over-
simplification, we might claim that the Shema is for Jews what the
Lord's Prayer is for Christians. In the present context, we may note
that both the Shema and the Lord's Prayer come from texts in the
Bible. A traditional prayer, like a proverb, is normally a fixed-phrase
genre. In other words, it is recited exactly the same way each time it is
uttered.

We find a version of the Shema in Deuteronomy:

> *Hear, O Israel: The Lord our God is one Lord: And thou shalt love the
> Lord thy God with all thine **heart**, and with all thy **soul**, and with all thy
> **might** (Deut. 6:4–5).*

There is an echo of the Shema later in Deuteronomy:

> *And it shall come to pass, if ye shall hearken diligently unto my com-
> mandments which I command you this day, to love the Lord your God and
> to serve him with all your **heart** and with all your **soul** (Deut. 11:13).*

A cursory comparison of the two Deuteronomy versions of the Shema
shows that the second one refers to "heart" and "soul" but does not
mention "might," which is an additional element in the first version.
The importance of the Shema is, interestingly enough, signaled by the
fact that Jesus, who was, of course, Jewish, referred to it as the "first of
all the commandments":

> *And one of the scribes came, and . . . asked him, Which is the first com-
> mandment of all? And Jesus answered him, The first of all the command-
> ments is, Hear, O Israel: The Lord our God is one Lord: And thou shalt love
> the Lord thy God with all thy **heart**, and with all thy **soul**, and with all
> thy **mind**, and with all thy **strength**: this is the first commandment (Mark
> 12:28–30).*

It is apparent that the version of the Shema cited by Jesus is somewhat longer than the ones appearing in Deuteronomy. It is also certainly longer than the versions of the first of the Ten Commandments given by God to Moses: *"I am the Lord thy God which have brought thee out of the land of Egypt out of the house of bondage"* (Exod. 20:2, Lev. 19:3, Num. 15:41, Deut. 5:6). There is no allusion in the Shema text to the escape from bondage in Egypt. Irrespective of the Shema's possible relationship to the first of the Ten Commandments, the two versions in Deuteronomy and one cited by Jesus by themselves demonstrate multiple existence and variation. "Heart," "soul," and "might" are different from "heart" and "soul," and both series are different from "heart," "soul," "mind," and "strength."

The Lord's Prayer

As there is surprising variation in the Jewish Shema, there is similar variation in the Christian Lord's Prayer. Before citing biblical texts, let me give a version in contemporary Anglo-American usage:

> Our Father **who** art in heaven
> Hallowed be thy name.
> Thy kingdom come.
> Thy will be done **on** earth,
> As it is in heaven.
> Give us this day
> our daily bread.
> Forgive us our trespasses,
> as we forgive those
> who trespass against us.
> Lead us not into temptation,
> but deliver us from evil.
> For thine is the kingdom,
> and the power, and the glory,
> forever, Amen.

This version is closest to the text cited in Matthew:

*After this manner therefore pray ye: Our Father **which** art in heaven, Hallowed be thy name. Thy kingdom come. Thy will be done **in** earth as it* *is in heaven. Give us this day our daily bread.* **And forgive us our debts, as we forgive our debtors.** *And lead us not into temptation, but deliver us from evil: For thine is the kingdom, and the power, and the glory, for ever. Amen.* **For if ye forgive men their trespasses, your heavenly Father will also forgive you: But if ye forgive not men their trespasses, neither will your Father forgive your trespasses** (Matt. 6:9–15).

The version in Luke is definitely cognate:

> *And he said unto them, When ye pray, say, Our Father which art in heaven. Hallowed be thy name. Thy kingdom come. Thy will be done, as in heaven, so in earth. Give us day by day our daily bread. And forgive us our sins; for we also forgive every one that is indebted to us. And lead us not into temptation; but deliver us from evil* (Luke 11:2–4).

There is a minor sequential variation in the placement of "heaven" and "earth." In marked contrast, the version in Mark is fragmentary at best. Most of the familiar felicitous phraseology is absent:

> *Therefore I say unto you, What things soever ye desire, when ye pray, believe that ye receive them, and ye shall have them. And when ye stand praying, forgive, if you have aught against any; that your Father also which is in heaven may forgive you your trespasses. But if ye do not forgive, neither will your Father which is in heaven forgive your trespasses* (Mark 11:24–26).

The very last portion of Mark's version is very similar to the final section of Matthew's version, but Mark's version is only a feeble echo of the fuller texts of this important prayer.

Perhaps the reader is somewhat surprised to discover that the version of Lord's Prayer so commonly known is not found with precisely the same identical wording in the Bible. This is a prime instance of how oral tradition has been adjudged superior to the written text. It is the oral version, after all, that is recited, not the written versions in Matthew, Mark, and Luke. The same situation obtains in the case of the so-called Golden Rule. The oral version current in the twentieth century is: "Do unto others as you would have others (or them) do unto you." Note the slight variation in the two oral versions, so typical of folklore. Similar expressions have been reported from non-Western cultures (cf. Hertzler 1933–34), but it is generally assumed that the oral version cited comes from the New Testament. Let us consider the versions in Matthew and Luke:

> *Therefore all things whatsoever ye would that men should do to you, do ye even so to them: for this is the law and the prophets* (Matt. 7:12).

> *And as ye would that men should do to you, do ye also to them likewise* (Luke 6:31).

Again, it appears that the common oral version does not correspond exactly to the versions in the Bible. The folk adaptation of materials **from** the Bible constitutes yet another aspect of the study of folklore and the Bible (cf. Utley 1945). This explains why, for example, the folk conceptualization of the life of Jesus draws upon elements from all four Gospels to create a traditional composite story that corresponds in all its detail to no one of them (cf. Dundes 1980).

The differences in the versions of the Lord's Prayer and the Golden Rule remind us that there are simply too many variations in the four Gospels to list them all. It would be laborious and tedious to do so. Moreover, it is really not necessary to mention them all to prove that we are dealing with four versions of one basic narrative, versions that were once in oral tradition and that even after being recorded continue to exhibit telltale variation. The variation cannot be explained simply as resulting from scribal errors or mistranslations. There are fundamental differences in the four versions, differences that are entirely to be expected when encountering oral tradition or what was once oral tradition.

Still More Duplicate Texts

The following examples are meant to be illustrative and not exhaustive. One of the most important rituals in Catholicism is the sacrament of Holy Communion, or the Eucharist. It is based on a specific event in the life of Jesus, an event in which Jesus gave verbal instruction to his disciples as to what they were to do. Not surprisingly, however, there are different versions of this event and the verbal instructions.

> *And as they were eating, Jesus took bread, and blessed it, and brake it, and gave it to the disciples, and said, Take, eat; this is my body. And he*

> *took the cup, and gave thanks, and gave it to them, saying,* **Drink ye all of**
> **it;** *For this is my blood of the new testament, which is shed for many* **for**
> **remission of sins.** *But I say unto you, I will not drink henceforth of this*
> *fruit of the vine, until that day when I drink it new* **with you** *in my Father's*
> *kingdom* (Matt. 26:26–29).

Mark's version is quite similar, with only a few minor variations:

> *And as they did eat, Jesus took bread, and blessed, and brake it, and gave*
> *it to them, and said, Take, eat; this is my body. And he took the cup, and*
> *when he had given thanks, he gave it to them: and they all drank of it. And*
> *he said unto them, This is my blood of the new testament, which is shed for*
> *many. Verily I say unto you, I will drink no more of the fruit of the vine,*
> *until that day that I drink it new in the kingdom of God* (Mark 14:22–25).

Mark's version has no mention of *"remission of sins"*; the words *"Drink
ye all of it"* do not appear; and the phrase *"with you"* is absent.
Luke offers the following version:

> *For I say unto you, I will not drink of the fruit of the vine, until the*
> *kingdom of God shall come. And he took bread, and gave thanks, and brake*
> *it, and gave unto them, saying, This is my body which is given for you:* **this**
> **do in remembrance of me.** *Likewise also the cup after supper, saying, This*
> *cup is the new testament in my blood, which is shed* **for you** (Luke 22:18–
> 20).

In Luke's version, we have a sequential variation inasmuch as the re-
fusal to drink the fruit of the vine **precedes** rather than follows verbal
instructions. Also the blood is not shed *"for many"* but *"for you."* And
Luke's version contains the additional classic line *"This do in remembrance of me,"* which does not occur in either Matthew or Mark.

John's account comes earlier than at the Last Supper, and the wording is very different:

> *I am the living bread which came down from heaven: if any man eat of*
> *this bread, he shall live for ever: and the bread that I will give is my flesh*
> *which I will give for the life of the world. . . . Then Jesus said unto them,*
> *Verily, verily, I say unto you, Except ye eat the flesh of the Son of man, and*
> *drink his blood, ye have no life in you. Whoso eateth my flesh, and drinketh*
> *my blood, hath eternal life; and I will raise him up at the last day. For my*
> *flesh is meat indeed, and my blood is drink indeed. He that eateth my flesh,*
> *and drinketh my blood, dwelleth in me, and I in him* (John 6:51, 53–56).

In 1 Corinthians we find another version, reminiscent of the one in Luke:

> *That the Lord Jesus, the same night in which he was betrayed, took bread: And when he had given thanks, he brake it, and said, Take, eat; this is my body, which is broken for you:* **this do in remembrance of me.** *After the same manner also he took the cup, when he had supped, saying, This cup is the new testament in my blood: this do ye, as oft as ye drink it,* **in remembrance of me.** *For as often as ye eat this bread, and drink this cup, ye do show the Lord's death till he come* (1 Cor. 11:23–26).

The Corinthians version has the *"in remembrance of me"* phrase found in Luke but not in Matthew or Mark. On the other hand, the Corinthians version has the *"Take, eat, this is my body"* line that is found in Matthew and Mark but not in Luke. In that sense, the Corinthians text represents a composite version with elements from Matthew, Mark, and Luke.

On the subject of instructions, we may observe that Luke gives two accounts of Jesus' instructions to his disciples as to what to take with them in the way of provisions prior to going out to preach.

> *And he said unto them, Taking nothing for your journey, neither staves, nor scrip, neither bread, neither money: neither have two coats apiece* (Luke 9:3).

> *Carry neither purse, nor scrip, nor shoes: and salute no man by the way* (Luke 10:4).

There is another allusion in Luke to this instruction:

> *And he said unto them, When I sent you without purse and scrip, and shoes, lacked ye any thing? And they said, Nothing* (Luke 22:35).

We may compare these versions with the accounts in Matthew and Mark.

> *Provide neither gold, nor silver, nor brass in your purses; Nor scrip for your journey, neither two coats, neither shoes, nor yet staves* (Matt. 10:9–10).

> *And commanded them that they should take nothing for their journey, save a staff only; no scrip, no bread, no money in their purse: But be shod with sandals; and not put on two coats* (Mark 6:9).

We find the usual sorts of variation in terms of the items listed, but there can be no question of the cognation of the passages. There is obvious consensus in the detail of not taking two coats. However, there are also the inevitable discrepancies. Matthew and Luke dictate shoelessness, whereas Mark requires sandals. More striking perhaps is the difference between forbidding staves in Matthew and Luke and specifically taking a staff in Mark.

I must stress that it is not just that the four Gospels are four versions of the same narrative, but that there are multiple forms **within** an individual Gospel. Consider the following two passages from Matthew:

> *And if thy right eye offend thee, pluck it out, and cast it from thee: for it is profitable for thee that one of thy members should perish, and not that thy whole body should be cast into hell. And if thy right hand offend thee, cut it off, and cast it from thee: for it is profitable for thee that one of thy members should perish, and not that thy whole body should be cast into hell* (Matt. 5:29–30).

> *Wherefore if thy hand or thy foot offend thee, cut them off, and cast them from thee: it is better for thee to enter into life halt or maimed, rather than having two hands or two feet to be cast into everlasting fire. And if thine eye offend thee, pluck it out, and cast it from thee: it is better for thee to enter into life with one eye rather than having two eyes to be cast into hell fire* (Matt. 18:8–9).

These two passages are definitely cognate, but they provide a casebook illustration of the nature of variation. The sequence is altered with eyes preceding limbs in the first passage and limbs preceding eyes in the second. A hand in the first version becomes a hand and a foot in the second, and there are other variations in the phrasing of the two texts. A slightly more elaborated version is to be found in Mark:

> *And if thy hand offend thee, cut it off: it is better for thee to enter into life maimed, than having two hands to go into hell, into the fire that never shall be quenched: Where their worm dieth not, and the fire is not quenched. And if thy foot offend thee, cut it off: it is better for thee to enter halt into life, than having two feet to be cast into hell, into the fire that never shall be quenched: Where their worm dieth not, and the fire is not quenched. And if thine eye offend thee, pluck it out: it is better for thee to enter into the kingdom of God with one eye, than having two eyes to be cast into hell fire: Where their worm dieth not, and the fire is not quenched* Mark 9:43–48).

This is the same passage, but here there is a definite tripartite structure with a hand, foot, and eye sequence. Furthermore, there is a repeated "worm" formula to separate the different elements. Such repetition bears all the earmarks of folklore. Sure enough, we find the very same formula in the Old Testament:

> *And they shall go forth, and look upon the carcasses of the men that have transgressed against me: for their worm shall not die, neither shall their fire be quenched: and they shall be an abhorring unto all flesh* (Isa. 66:24).

It is probably worth remarking that this is not the kind of stylistic variation that troubles some readers of the Bible. Rather it is the variation that tends to obscure potential historical facts that most bothers some biblical scholars. Speaking of rabbinic stories, Bultmann observes "That they cannot possibly be taken as historical reports is shown in the first place by the variants of certain stories" (1963:50). On the other hand, the existence of two versions of the flood myth cannot be used to "prove" that a flood never occurred. Still, it is true that variants do present problems for historians. For example, at one point, preferential treatment is requested for two of the twelve disciples, James and John. At issue is whether James and John asked for this favor from Jesus themselves or whether it was their mother who approached Jesus with the request. Here are two versions of the incident:

> **And James and John, the sons of Zebedee, come unto him,** *saying, Master, we would that thou shouldest do for us whatsoever we shall desire. And he said unto them, What would ye that I should do for you? They said unto him, Grant unto us that we may sit, one on thy right hand, and the other on thy left hand, in thy glory* (Mark 10:35–37).

> **Then came to him the mother of Zebedee's children** *with her sons, worshipping him, and desiring a certain thing of him. And he said unto her, What wilt thou? She said unto him, Grant that these my two sons may sit, the one on thy right hand, and the other on the left in thy kingdom* (Matt. 20:20–21).

Of course, it is perfectly possible that **both** the sons **and** the mother made the same request of Jesus. On the other hand, it does look like two versions of the same incident.

Similarly, what did the centurion say as he watched Jesus die on the cross? According to Matthew (27:54), he said, *"Truly this was the Son of God.*" But according to Luke (23:47), the centurion said, *"Certainly this was a righteous man."* Again, the centurion could well have expressed both sentiments, but there is clearly a disparity insofar as each account gives just one utterance.

Perhaps posing more of a problem for the historian are the diverse accounts of the wording of the inscription placed above Jesus' head when he was on the cross. Matthew (27:37) reports, *"And set up over his head his accusation written 'This is Jesus the King of the Jews.'"* Mark (25:26) says, *"And the superscription of his accusation was written over, 'The King of the Jews.'"* Luke (23:38) offers a combination of the two: *"And a superscription also was written over him in letters of Greek, and Latin, and Hebrew 'This is the King of the Jews.'"* John (19:19) differs: *"And Pilate wrote a title, and put it on the cross. And the writing was, 'Jesus of Nazareth the King of the Jews.'"* So we have four versions of the inscription, no two of them verbatim identical:

> *This is Jesus the King of the Jews*
> *The King of the Jews*
> *This is the King of the Jews*
> *Jesus of Nazareth the King of the Jews*

One wonders if the difference between referring to Christ as "Jesus" versus "Jesus of Nazareth," a distinction noted earlier in the two accounts of Paul's conversion on the road to Damascus, might be analogous to the J and E voices in the Old Testament, so labeled because of different names for God.

There are also different versions of Jesus' last words before dying on the cross. Both Matthew and Mark indicate that *"about the ninth hour"* Jesus cried with a loud voice, *"My God, my God, why hast thou forsaken me?"* (Matt. 27:40; Mark 15:34). But both are silent with respect to the content of his very last utterance on the cross:

> *Jesus, when he had cried again with a loud voice, yielded up the ghost* (Matt. 27:50).

> *And Jesus cried with a loud voice, and gave up the ghost* (Mark 15:37).

But both Luke and John are more specific:

And when Jesus had cried with a loud voice, he said, Father, into thy
hands I commend my spirit: and having said thus, he gave up the ghost
(Luke 23:46).

He said, It is finished: and he bowed his head, and gave up the ghost
(John 19:30).

If Jesus uttered any of these last words, it is certainly curious that he
chose that strategic moment to quote from the Psalms of the Old Testament. Psalm 22 begins, *"My God, my God, why hast thou forsaken
me?"* and the fifth verse of Psalm 31 begins, *"Into thine hand I commit
my spirit."* The citation of the initial line of Psalm 22 in Matthew
(27:46) is not accidental inasmuch as a preceding verse also echoes one
from the same psalm:

He trusted in God; let him deliver him now, if he will have him. . . .
(Matt. 27:43).

He trusted in the Lord that he would deliver him: let him deliver him,
seeing he delighted in him (Ps. 22:8).

Conclusion

The final words of Jesus on the cross may serve as a hint that I should
bring this investigation to a close. If I wanted to encapsulate my argument in the form of a syllogism, I might propose the following:

1. Folklore is characterized by multiple existence and variation.
2. The Bible is permeated by multiple existence and variation.
3. The Bible is folklore!

What are the implications of this conclusion? First of all, I believe Jesus
would have understood my argument. Why do I think so? The Phari-
sees and the Sadducees tried to tempt Jesus into showing them *"a sign
from heaven"* (Matt. 16:1). Jesus responded by citing a weather superstition: *"He answered and said unto them, When it is evening, ye say, It
will be fair weather: for the sky is red. And in the morning it will be foul
weather today: for the sky is red and lowering"* (Matt. 16:2–3). This su-

perstition is still in tradition. Typical modern versions are: "Red sky at night, sailors' (shepherds') delight; Red sky in the morning, sailors (shepherds) take warning." Indeed, the text in the Bible may serve as a useful *terminus ante quem* for the superstition. But my point here is to call attention to the use of the quotative "ye say" that shows that Jesus was referring to something already known to his audience. That is, Jesus himself recognized that the item was already traditional at that time. In sum, he realized that oral tradition was a source of folk knowledge. The acknowledgment by Jesus of oral tradition is also signaled by his repeated use of such introductory formulas as *"Ye have **heard** that it was **said** by them of old time"* (Matt. 5:21, 27, 33) and *"Ye have **heard** that it hath been **said**"* (Matt. 5:38, 43).

The occurrence of a traditional superstition in the New Testament reminds us that there are numerous examples of individual items of folklore in the Bible, items whose authenticity as folklore can be easily documented by citing versions **outside** the Bible. This is the older folkloristic approach to the Bible, the approach employed by Frazer and others. And it is true that there are countless examples. There is Samson's neck riddle *"Out of the eater came forth meat, and out of the strong came forth sweetness"* (Judg. 14:14; for representative discussions, see Torcszyner 1924:126–35 and Porter 1962); there is the use of a tongue twister involving the *s* and *sh* alternation *"Say now Shibboleth: and he said Sibboleth"* (Judg. 12:6), a device comparable to those used in World War II to distinguish Dutch and German speakers; and there is even a traditional children's game.

A common "it" game with various names—in England it is called "Stroke the Baby," among other designations—has "it" facing a wall or blindfolded. Another child strikes "it" on the back or on the buttocks. "It" is supposed to guess who hit him. If he guesses correctly, then he and the hitter exchange places. This is a very old game. There is a picture on the wall of an ancient Egyptian tomb that dates the game at circa 2000 B.C. (Opie and Opie 1969:294). What has this to do with the Bible? After Jesus has been taken prisoner, the soldiers present mock him, and they do so by pretending to play this very game. There are three versions:

> *Then did they spit in his face, and buffeted him; and others smote him with the palms of their hands, Saying, Prophesy unto us, thou Christ, Who is he that smote thee?* (Matt. 26:67–68).

And some began to spit on him, and to cover his face, and to buffet him, and to say unto him, Prophesy: and the servants did strike him with the palms of their hands (Mark 14:65).

And the men that held Jesus mocked him, and smote him. And when they had blindfolded him, they struck him on the face, and asked him, saying Prophesy, who is it that smote thee? (Luke 22:63–64).

There seems little doubt that this is an allusion to a traditional guessing game, a game that antedates the Bible.

It is not all that difficult to find such parallels to elements in the Bible (cf. for the Old Testament, Frazer 1918; Irvin 1978; Matthews and Benjamin 1991; for the New Testament, Bultmann 1963:106, 204, 234–38; Martin 1988; Cartlidge and Dungan 1994). Among such parallels are Egyptian texts, one of which is the teaching or wisdom of Amen-em-ope. There can be no question that there are cognates. The Egyptian text dates from somewhere between the tenth and sixth centuries B.C. and is presumed to be older than the corresponding Old Testament proverbs (Pritchard 1950:421; cf. Simpson 1926, Keimer 1926–27, Eissfeldt 1965:474, Ruffle 1977, Matthews and Benjamin 1991:189–98). Here are some samples:

(from Amen-em-ope)

Give thy ears, hear what is said,	*Bow down thine ear, and hear the*
Give thy heart to understand them.	*words of the wise, and apply thine*
	heart unto my knowledge (Prov.
	22:17).

Another parallel concerns the advice not to seek after riches because they invariably fly away like birds.

Cast not thy heart in pursuit of riches	*Wilt thou set thine eyes upon that*
. . . they have made themselves wings	*which is not? for riches certainly make*
like geese and are flown away to the	*themselves wings; they fly away as an*
heavens. (from Amen-em-ope)	*eagle toward heaven* (Prov. 23:5).

Finally, there is a warning against eating the bread of someone with the evil eye. If one eats such bread, one is likely to vomit it.

Be not greedy for the property of a poor	*Eat thou not the bread of him that*
man, Nor hunger for his bread. . . . His	*hath an evil eye, neither desire thou his*

heart is perverted by his belly. The
mouthful of bread great thou
swallowest and vomitest up, And art
emptied of thy good (from Amen-em-
ope).

dainty meats: For as he thinketh in his
heart, so is he: Eat and drink, saith he
to thee; but his heart is not with thee.
The morsel which thou hast eaten shalt
thou vomit up, and lose thy sweet
words (Prov. 23:6–8).

There are parallels from other ancient cultures as well. One example would be a proverb found in Ecclesiastes 5:12: *"The sleep of a laboring man is sweet, whether he eat little or much: but the abundance of the rich will not suffer him to sleep."* Compare that proverb with the following Sumerian proverb: *"He who has silver is happy, he who has grain feels comfortable, but he who has livestock cannot sleep"* (Alster 1997:84, 268, 298, 311). Another proverb in Ecclesiastes (4:12) proclaims that *"a threefold cord is not quickly broken."* This is undoubtedly cognate with the Sumerian proverb *"The three-ply rope will not easily be cut"* (Hallo 1988:35). Sumerian culture antedates that of the Old Testament (Hallo 1988). I mention this lest the unwary reader wrongly assume that the Sumerians learned the proverb from the Bible! The Sumerian proverbs date from approximately 2600 B.C. In addition to obvious Egyptian and Sumerian parallels, there are also Aramaic cognates. For example, one of the proverbs of Ahiqar from the fifth century B.C., if not earlier, is: *"Let not the rich man say, "In my riches I am glorious"* (Lindenberger 1983:207). This is surely the same proverb as *"Let not the rich man glory in his riches"* (Jer. 9:23).

In the same way, one can locate tale types in the Bible. There seems to be a version of Aarne-Thompson tale type 910F, The Quarreling Sons and the Bundle of Twigs. Peasant puts twigs together and cannot break them. Separately they are easily broken. His sons apply the lesson. It appears in Ezekiel 37:15–22, in which the quarreling tribes of Israel are likened to sticks that if put together can be undivided as "one nation." Similarly there seems to be a version of Aarne-Thompson tale type 293, Debate of the Belly and the Members. Debate as to their usefulness. All are mutually useful. This occurs in 1 Corinthians 12:12–26. And, of course, there is Aarne-Thompson tale type 926, Judgment of Solomon, the title of which reflects the biblical version of the story (1 Kings 3:16–28). This is an ancient Indo-European folktale. It was known in India, where it was a Jataka tale (cf. Grey 1990:76–77). But this kind of research is atomistic and piecemeal. It is not uninteresting, but I have purposely avoided using sources outside the Bible to "prove" that it is folklore, instead limiting my discussion to internal textual evidence. And I have not confined my investigation to just the Old or just the New Testament. It is my contention that the entire Bible qualifies as folklore.

If I am right about my claim that the Bible is folklore, what are the implications of this finding? I believe that it may represent a new paradigm with which to appreciate and better understand the Bible. There have been many approaches to the Bible: the Bible as religious document, the Bible as history (cf. Keller 1981); and the Bible as literature (cf. Alter 1981, Alter and Kermode 1987, Minor 1992, and Powell 1992). To these, I suggest a new approach: **the Bible as folklore.** It is not that one should cease taking a religious or historical or literary tack in reading the Bible, but only that one should realize that the object of such investigations is folklore.

One obvious advantage of utilizing a folkloristic paradigm, for example, for those with a historical bias, is that long-standing problems or difficulties can now be seen in quite a new light. The term "light" reminds us of a case in point. God creates light (Genesis 1:3) before he gets around to creating the sun and moon (Genesis 1:16). This may be a problem for the logician or the historian, but for the folklorist it is just a matter of two or more conflicting oral versions that have been unwisely conflated. Another "problem" is that the Pentateuch, the first five books of the Old Testament, was alleged to have been written by Moses. Yet the last chapter of Deuteronomy, the fifth book, contains a detailed account of Moses' own death, his funeral as well as his obituary (Deuteronomy 24:5–8). We have already discussed how questions of attribution abound in the Bible. Did God or did Moses write down the Ten Commandments? Is Isaiah or Micah responsible for the "swords into plowshares" metaphor? In most instances, the author of folklore texts is unknown. "Anonymous" is usually listed as the author of such texts. Authorship in the case of folklore is almost always unknowable or irrelevant. Who was the first to compose the plot of "Cinderella"? No one knows or is ever likely to know. The point is that once we recognize the Bible as folklore, questions of authorship become less of an issue.

Biblical scholars have long recognized the existence of duplicate texts or multiforms in the Bible, but they have failed to fully appreciate the significance of those multiple versions. In folkloristic terms, it is not always possible to reconcile competing versions of a legend or to choose one version of a proverb over another. Instead, each version must be understood and evaluated on its own merits. Consequently, many of the "problems" facing Bible historians and critics turn out to be nonproblems from a folkloristic perspective. There seems to be an endless number of tracts and books that attempt to reconcile "seeming" or "apparent" or "alleged" discrepancies or contradictions in the Bible (Arndt 1987, Archer, 1982, Burr, 1987, De Haan, 1952, DeHoff 1950, Geisler and Howe, 1992, Haley 1977, Johnson 1983, Richards 1993, Torrey 1907, Tuck 1891, Williams 1924). Most of the writers of such tracts are totally committed to the idea of the "inerrancy" of the Bible, by which they mean that the Bible by definition cannot contain anything untrue. The governing paradigmatic syllogism is:

> God Cannot Err.
> The Bible Is the Word of God.
> Therefore, the Bible Cannot Err.
> (Geisler and Howe 1992:11)

In the case of the New Testament, there has been a long series of attempts to "harmonize" the Gospels, that is, to smooth out the "apparent" contradictions. One of the earliest was written by the second-century Christian writer Tatian. In his *Diatessarion,* compiled circa 172, Tatian attempted to weave the four Gospels into one continuous coherent narrative. To accomplish this, he had to eliminate duplications, reconcile contradictions, and produce composite combinations of parallel passages (Petersen 1994:1). Two centuries later, Saint Augustine, for example, also sought to refute such criticisms of the New Testament when he wrote *The Harmony of the Evangelists* circa A.D. 400. And there continue to be efforts to eliminate divergences in the essential story line, for example, Orville E. Daniel's *A Harmony of the Four Gospels: The New International Version* (1986). The "harmony" is achieved in part by privileging just one of the four Gospels at various points in order to give the impression that there is a single-stranded historical plot. For that matter, the individual Gospels themselves may be the results of harmonizing efforts. For instance, Luke begins his Gospel with a reference to the **"many"** who have *"taken in hand to set forth in order a declaration of those things which are most surely believed among us,"* some of the "many" having been "eyewitnesses," but Luke indicates that his *"perfect understanding of all things from the very first"* allows him to put these accounts *"in order"* (Luke 1:1–2). The final words of the Gospel of John also suggest that his testimony represents just a tiny fraction of the unrecorded oral traditions available to him:

And there also many other things which Jesus did, the which, if they should be written every one, I suppose that even the world itself could not contain the books that should be written (John 21:25).

But harmonizing the four Gospels entails disregarding the contents of parallel passages in one or more of the other three Gospels. Although the vast majority of harmonizing efforts have been devoted to the Gospels, there have also been attempts to apply the same technique to duplicate texts in the Old Testament, such as William Day Crockett's *A Harmony of Samuel, Kings and Chronicles* (1985). From the perspective resulting from this book, the point is that with multiple versions of folklore, variation is the norm. What are labeled discrepancies or contradictions are nothing more than the predictable results of oral transmission and tradition. With folklore, it is rarely possible to say that any one version of a legend or folktale is "better" or more authentic than another version. Yet the historical Jesus and the *ipsissima verba Jesu*—the "authentic words of Jesus"—remain an unattainable quest object for many scholars. In 1985, the Jesus Seminar was formed, and in their 1993 book *The Five Gospels: The Search for the Authentic Words of Jesus,* a collective effort was made to differentiate strands in the New Testament. The strands were marked by means of a color code: red meant that Jesus undoubtedly said it; pink (a weakened form of red) meant Jesus probably said something like it; gray meant Jesus did not say it but the ideas expressed are close to his ideas; and black meant that Jesus did not say it. The members of the Jesus Seminar certainly acknowledged the existence and influence of oral tradition, but their goal in part was to distinguish what Jesus said from what they term "common lore." One of their announced assumptions was that "Jesus' characteristic talk was distinctive—it can usually be distinguished from common lore. Otherwise it is futile to search for the authentic words of Jesus" (Funk and Hoover 1993:30). This goal is predicated upon the idea that the Bible itself, although it may contain elements of folklore, is not itself folklore. It is, to put it another way, a continuation of the "folklore in the Bible" tradition. If there is folklore in the Bible, then it would in theory be possible to weed it out, thereby leaving only authentic history or nonfolklore to consider. The argument I am proposing is different. If the entire Bible is folklore, codified oral tradition, then there can be no way of weeding out the folklore. If one weeded out the folklore, virtually nothing would be left. The Jesus Seminar has also published a sequel entitled *The Acts of Jesus* (Funk 1998) in which the same color-coding scheme is utilized to distinguish a gamut of events ranging from those that presumably actually occurred (red) to those that are regarded as purely fictive (black). It is by no means clear, however, how any sort of subjective voting mechanism, even by a group of purported Bible experts, can reliably ascertain which portions of the Bible are to be regarded as fact and which are to be dismissed as fiction.

The multiple versions of nearly every major episode in both the Old and New Testaments—the creation of woman, the flood, the wife-sister subterfuge, the Ten Commandments, the names of the twelve tribes of Israel, the names of the twelve disciples, the Sermon on the Mount, the Shema, the Lord's Prayer, the words inscribed on the cross, and the last words of Jesus before giving up the ghost, among scores of examples—attest to the folkloricity of the Bible. There is no one fixed text, but only multiple texts that manifest extraordinary variation in number, name, and sequence. The Bible may well be "the greatest book in the world" (Siamakis 1997:8) and "the most important book in the world" (Richards 1993:7), but it is truly folklore, and it is high time that it is recognized as such.

Bibliography

Aarne, Antti, and Stith Thompson. 1961. *The Types of the Folktale.* 2nd rev. FF Communications No. 184. Helsinki: Academia Scientiarum Fennica.

Ahlström, G. W. 1966. "Oral and Written Transmission: Some Considerations." *Harvard Theological Review* 598:69–81.

Alster, Bendt. 1997. *Proverbs of Ancient Sumer: The World's Earliest Proverb Collections.* 2 vols. Bethesda, Md.: CDL Press.

Alter, Robert. 1981. *The Art of Biblical Narrative.* New York: Basic Books.

Alter, Robert, and Frank Kermode, eds. 1987. *The Literary Guide to the Bible.* Cambridge: Harvard University Press.

Anderson, G. W. 1950. "Some Aspects of the Uppsala School of Old Testament Study." *Harvard Theological Review* 43:239–56.

Anderson, Janice Capel. 1985. "Double and Triple Stories, The Implied Reader, and Redundancy in Matthew." *Semeia* 31:71–89.

Aranda, Mariano Gómez. 1997. "Transmisión oral y transmisión escrita: La Biblia Hebrea." In *Entre La Palabra y el Texto,* ed. Luis Díaz G. Viana and Matilde Fernández Montes, 245–68. Madrid: Consejo Superior de Investigaciones Científicas.

Archer, Gleason L. 1982. *Encyclopedia of Bible Difficulties.* Grand Rapids, Mich.: Zondervan.

Arndt, William. 1987. *Bible Difficulties & Seeming Contradictions.* St. Louis: Concordia.

Augustine, Saint. 1873. *The Works of Aurelius Augustine,* Vol. VIII. *The Sermon on the Mount, and The Harmony of the Evangelists.* Edinburgh: T. & T. Clark.

Bailey, Kenneth E. 1991. "Informal Controlled Oral Tradition and the Synoptic Gospels." *Asia Journal of Theology* 5:34–54.

Boman, Thorlief. 1967. *Die Jesus-Überlieferung im Lichte der neueren Volkskunde.* Göttingen: Vandenhoeck & Ruprecht.

119

Brandes, Stanley. 1985. *Forty: The Age and the Symbol.* Knoxville: University of Tennessee Press.

Brewer, Derek. 1979. "The Gospels and the Laws of Folktale." *Folklore* 90:37–52.

Bultmann, Rudolf. 1963. *History of the Synoptic Tradition.* Peabody, Mass.: Hendrickson Publishers.

Burr, William Henry. 1987. *Self-Contradictions of the Bible.* Buffalo: Prometheus Books.

Cartlidge, David R., and David L. Dungan, eds. 1994. *Documents for the Study of the Gospels.* 2nd ed. Minneapolis: Fortress Press.

Clements, Ronald E. 1976. *One Hundred Years of Old Testament Interpretation.* Philadelphia: Westminster Press.

Crane, T. F. 1885. Sicilian Proverbs. *Lippincott's Magazine* 35:309–13.

Crockett, William Day. 1985. *A Harmony of Samuel, Kings, and Chronicles.* Grand Rapids, Mich.: Baker Book House.

Culley, R. C. 1963. "An Approach to the Problem of Oral Tradition." *Vetus Testamentum* 13:113–25.

Culley, Robert C. 1972. "Oral Tradition and Historicity." In *Studies on the Ancient Palestinian World.* ed. J. W. Wevers and D. B. Redford, 102–16. Toronto: University of Toronto Press.

———. 1976a. "Oral Tradition and the Old Testament: Some Recent Discussion." *Semeia* 5:1–33.

———. 1976b. *Studies in the Structure of Hebrew Narrative.* Philadelphia: Fortress Press.

———. 1986. "Oral Tradition and Biblical Studies." *Oral Tradition* 1:30–65.

———. 1992. *Themes and Variations: A Study of Action in Biblical Narrative.* Atlanta: Scholars Press.

Daniel, Orville E. 1986. *A Harmony of the Four Gospels: The New International Version.* Grand Rapids, Mich.: Baker Book House.

De Haan, M. R. 1952. *508 Answers to Bible Questions with Answers to Seeming Bible Contradictions.* Grand Rapids, Mich.: Zondervan.

DeHoff, George W. 1950. *Alleged Bible Contradictions Explained.* Murfreesboro, Tenn.: DeHoff Publications.

Dibelius, Martin. 1936. *A Fresh Approach to the New Testament and Early Christian Literature.* London: Ivor Nicholson and Watson.

———. 1965. *From Tradition to Gospel.* New York: Charles Scribner's Sons.

Doeve, J. W. 1957. "Le Rôle de la tradition orale dans la composition des evangiles synoptiques." In *La Formation des Évangiles,* 70–84. Louvain: Desclèe de Brouwer.

Dorson, Richard M. 1972. "The Debate over the Trustworthiness of Oral Traditional History." In *Folklore: Selected Essays,* ed. Richard M. Dorson, 199–224. Bloomington: Indiana University Press.

Dundes, Alan. 1980. "The Hero Pattern and the Life of Jesus." In *Interpreting Folklore,* ed. Alan Dundes, 223–61. Bloomington: Indiana University Press.

Dundes, Alan, ed. 1984. *Sacred Narrative: Readings in the Theory of Myth.* Berkeley: University of California Press.

———. 1988. *The Flood Myth.* Berkeley: University of California Press.

Eissfeldt, Otto. 1965. *The Old Testament: An Introduction.* New York: Harper and Row.

Engnell, Ivan. 1960. "Methodological Aspects of Old Testament Study." *Supplements to Vetus Testamentum* 6:13–30.

———. 1970. *Critical Essays on the Old Testament.* London: S.P.C.K.

Eusebius. 1965. *The History of the Church from Christ to Constantine.* London: Penguin Books.

Frayha, Anis. 1953. *Modern Lebanese Proverbs.* 2 vols. Beirut: American University of Beirut.

Frazer, James George. 1918. *Folklore in the Old Testament.* 3 vols. London: Macmillan.

Friedman, Richard Elliott. 1989. *Who Wrote the Bible?* New York: Harper and Row.

Funk, Robert, and the Jesus Seminar. 1998. *The Acts of Jesus: The Search for the Authentic Deeds of Jesus.* San Francisco: Harper.

Funk, Robert W., and Roy W. Hoover, et al. 1993. *The Five Gospels: The Search for the Authentic Words of Jesus.* New York: Macmillan.

Gandz, Solomon. 1935. "Oral Tradition in the Bible." In *Jewish Studies in Memory of George A. Kohut.* ed. Salo W. Baron and Alexander Marx, 248–69. New York: Alexander Kohut Memorial Foundation.

Gaster, Moses. 1919. "Folk-Lore in the Old Testament." *Folk-Lore* 30:71-76.

Geisler, Norman, and Thomas Howe. 1992. *When Critics Ask: A Popular Handbook on Bible Difficulties.* Grand Rapids, Mich.: Baker Book House.

Gibert, Pierre. 1979. *Une Théorie de la légende: Hermann Gunkel (1862–1932) et les légendes de la Bible.* Paris: Flammarion.

Gordis, Daniel H. 1985. "Lies, Wives and Sisters: The Wife-Sister Motif Revisited." *Judaism* 34:344–59.

Grey, Leslie. 1990. *A Concordance of Buddhist Birth Stories.* Oxford: Pali Text Society.

Gunkel, Hermann. 1964. *The Legends of Genesis.* New York: Schocken Books.

———. 1987. *The Folktale in the Old Testament.* Sheffield: Almond Press.

Güttegemanns, Erhardt. 1979. *Candid Questions Concerning Gospel Form Criticism.* Pittsburgh: The Pickwick Press.

Habel, Norman. 1971. *Literary Criticism of the Old Testament.* Philadelphia: Fortress Press.

Hahn, Ferdinand. 1987. "Zur Verschriftlichung mündlicher Tradition in der Bibel." *Zeitschrift für Religions- und Geistesgeschichte* 39:307–18.

Haley, John W. 1977. *Alleged Discrepancies of the Bible.* Grand Rapids, Mich.: Baker Book House.

Hallo, William W. 1988. "Sumerian Literature: Background to the Bible." *Bible Review* 4(3):28–38.

Hanson, R. P. C. 1962. *Tradition in the Early Church.* London: SCM Press.

Helms, Randel. 1988. *Gospel Fictions.* Buffalo: Prometheus Books.

Hempel, Johannes. 1938. "The Forms of Oral Tradition." In *Record and Revelation.* ed. H. Wheeler Robinson, 28–44. Oxford: Clarendon Press.

Henaut, Barry W. 1993. *Oral Tradition and the Gospels: The Problem of Mark 4.* Sheffield: Sheffield Academic Press.

Hertzler, Joyce O. 1933–34. "On Golden Rules." *International Journal of Ethics* 44:418–436.

Irvin, Dorothy. 1978. *Mytharion: The Comparison of Tales from the Old Testament and the Ancient Near East.* Kevelaer: Verlag Butzon & Bercker.

Johnson, Carl G. 1983. *So The Bible Is Full of Contradictions?* Grand Rapids, Mich.: New Hope Press.

Keimer, Ludwig. 1926–27. "The Wisdom of Amen-em-ope and the Proverbs of Solomon." *American Journal of Semitic Languages and Literatures* 43:8–21.

Kelber, Werner H. 1980. "Mark and Oral Tradition." *Semeia* 16:7–55.

———. 1983. *The Oral and the Written Gospel.* Philadelphia: Fortress Press.

Keller, Werner. 1981. *The Bible as History.* 2nd rev. New York: William Morrow.

Kirkpatrick, Patricia G. 1988. *The Old Testament and Folklore Study.* Sheffield: Sheffield Academic Press.

Klem, Herbert V. 1982. *Oral Communication of the Scripture: Insights from African Oral Art.* Pasadena: William Carey Library.

Kloppenborg, John S. 1994. *The Shape of Q: Signal Essays on the Sayings Gospel.* Philadelphia: Fortress Press.

Knight, Douglas. 1975. *Rediscovering the Traditions of Israel.* Rev. ed. Missoula: Scholars Press.

Koch, Klaus. 1969. *The Growth of the Biblical Tradition: The Form-Critical Method.* New York: Charles Scribner's Sons.

Lane Fox, Robin. 1993. *The Unauthorized Version: Truth and Fiction in the Bible.* New York: Vintage.

Leach, Edmund. 1983. "Anthropological Approaches to the Study of the Bible during the Twentieth Century." In *Structuralist Interpretations of Biblical Myth,* ed. Edmund Leach and D. Alan Aycock, 7–32. Cambridge: Cambridge University Press.

Lescot, R. 1937. "Proverbes et enigmes kurdes." *Revue des Études Islamiques* 11:307–50.

Lindenberger, James M. 1983. *The Aramaic Proverbs of Ahiqar.* Baltimore: Johns Hopkins University Press.

Lods, Adolphe. 1923. "Le Rôle de la tradition orale dans la formation des récits de l'Ancien Testament." *Revue de l'Histoire des Religions* 83:51–64.

Lord, Albert B. 1978. "The Gospels as Oral Traditional Literature." In *The Relationship Among the Gospels: An Interdisciplinary Dialogue*, ed. William O. Walker, Jr., 33–91. San Antonio: Trinity University Press.

Martin, Francis. 1988. *Narrative Parallels to the New Testament*. Atlanta: Scholars Press.

Matthews, Victor H., and Don C. Benjamin. 1991. *Old Testament Parallels: Laws and Stories from the Ancient Near East*. New York: Paulist Press.

Mieder, Wolfgang. 1998. *"A House Divided": From Biblical Proverb to Lincoln and Beyond*. Supplement Series of *Proverbium*, Vol. 2. Burlington: University of Vermont.

Milne, Pamela J. 1988. *Vladimir Propp and the Study of Structure in Hebrew Biblical Narrative*. Sheffield: Almond Press.

Minor, Mark. 1992. *Literary-Critical Approaches to the Bible: An Annotated Bibliography*. West Cornwall, Conn.: Locust Hill Press.

Neusner, Jacob. 1987. *Oral Tradition in Judaism: The Case of the Mishnah*. New York: Garland.

Niditch, Susan. 1987. *Underdogs and Tricksters: A Prelude to Biblical Folklore*. San Francisco: Harper and Row.

———. 1993. *Folklore and the Hebrew Bible*. Minneapolis: Fortress Press.

———. 1996. *Oral World and Written Word: Ancient Israelite Literature*. Louisville, Ky.: Westminster John Knox Press.

Niditch, Susan, ed. 1990. *Text and Tradition: The Hebrew Bible and Folklore*. Atlanta: Scholars Press.

Nielsen, Eduard. 1954. *Oral Tradition*. Chicago: Alec R. Allenson.

North, C. R. 1949–50. "The Place of Oral Tradition in the Growth of the Old Testament." *Expository Times* 61:292–96.

———. 1954–55. "Oral Tradition and Written Documents." *Expository Times* 66:39.

Ohler, Annemarie. 1969. *Mythologische elemente im Alten Testament*. Düsseldorf: Patmos-Verlag.

Opie, Iona, and Peter Opie. 1969. *Children's Games in Street and Playground*. Oxford: Clarendon Press.

Otzen, Benedikt, Hans Gottlieb, and Knud Jeppesen. 1980. *Myths in the Old Testament*. London: SCM Press.

Petersen, David L. 1973. "A Thrice-Told Tale: Genre, Theme, and Motif." *Biblical Research* 18:30–43.

Petersen, William L. 1994. *Tatian's Diatessarion: Its Creation, Dissemination, Significance, and History in Scholarship*. Leiden: E. J. Brill.

Porter, J. R. 1962. "Samson's Riddle: Judges XIV. 14, 18." *Journal of Theological Studies* 13: 106–109.

Powell, Mark Allan. 1992. *The Bible and Modern Literary Criticism: A Critical Assessment and Annotated Bibliography*. New York: Greenwood Press.

Pritchard, James B., ed. 1950. *Ancient Near Eastern Texts*. Princeton, N.J.: Princeton University Press.

Richards, Larry. 1993. *735 Baffling Bible Questions Answered.* Grand Rapids, Mich.: Fleming H. Revell.

Ringgren, Helmer. 1950–51. "Oral and Written Transmission in the O.T.: Some Observations." *Studia Theologia* 3:34–59.

Roberts, Warren E. 1994. *The Tale of the Kind and the Unkind Girls.* Detroit: Wayne State University Press.

Rogerson, J. W. 1974. *Myth in Old Testament Interpretation.* Berlin: De Gruyter.

Ruffle, John. 1977. "The Teaching of Amenemope and Its Connection with the Book of Proverbs." *Tyndale Bulletin* 28:29–68.

Saintyves, P. 1922. *Essais de folklore biblique: Magie, mythes et miracles dans l'Ancien et le Nouveau Testament.* Paris: Emile Nourry.

Schneeweis, Emil. 1983. Volkskundliches im Alten Testament. *Österreichische Zeitschrift für Volkskunde* 86:149–54.

Siamakis, Constantine. 1997. *Transmission of the Text of the Holy Bible.* Belmont, Mass.: Institute for Byzantine and Modern Greek Studies.

Simpson, D. C. 1926. The Hebrew Book of Proverbs and the Teaching of Amenophis. *Journal of Egyptian Archeology* 12:232–39.

Stevenson, Sinclair, Mrs. 1920. *The Rites of the Twice-Born.* London: Oxford University Press.

Stuhlmueller, Carroll. 1958. "The Influence of Oral Tradition upon Exegesis and the Senses of Scripture." *Catholic Biblical Quarterly* 20:299–326.

Teeple, Howard M. 1970. "The Oral Tradition That Never Existed." *Journal of Biblical Literature* 89:56–68.

Torcszyner, Harry. 1924. "The Riddle in the Bible." *Hebrew Union College Annual* 1:125–49.

Torrey, R. A. 1907. *Difficulties and Alleged Errors and Contradictions in the Bible.* Chicago: Moody Press.

Tuck, Robert. 1891. *A Handbook of Scientific and Literary Bible Difficulties.* New York: Thomas Whittaker.

Tucker, Gene M. 1971. *Form Criticism of the Old Testament.* Philadelphia: Fortress Press.

Utley, Francis Lee. 1945. "The Bible of the Folk." *California Folklore Quarterly* 4:1–7.

Van der Ploeg, J. 1947. "Le Rôle de la tradition orale dans la transmission du texte de l'Ancien Testament." *Revue Biblique* 5–41.

Vansina, Jan. 1985. *Oral Tradition as History.* Madison: University of Wisconsin Press.

Widengren, Geo. 1959. "Oral Tradition and Written Literature among the Hebrews in the Light of Arabic Evidence with Special Regard to Prose Narratives." *Acta Orientalia* 23:201–62.

Willi, Thomas. 1971. *Herders Beitrag zum Verstehen des Alten Testaments.* Tübingen: J. C. B. Mohr.

Williams, George. 1924. *Supposed Bible Contradictions Harmonized.* London: Chas. Thynne & Jarvis.

Willis, John T. 1970. "I. Engnell's Contributions to Old Testament Scholarship." *Theologische Zeitschrift* 26:385–94.

Zlotnick, Dov. 1984–85. "Memory and the Integrity of the Oral Tradition." *Journal of the Ancient Near Eastern Society* 16–17:229–41.

Index

About the Author

Alan Dundes is known as one of the world's leading authorities on folklore. In more than thirty books he has unveiled the meanings in the oral traditions of many cultures. He lives in Berkeley, where he is professor of anthropology and folklore at the University of California.